COPING WITH MALE MID-LIFE

A Systematic Analysis Using Literature as a Data Source

Sharan B. Merriam

UNIVERSITY
PRESS OF
AMERICA

Copyright © 1980 by
University Press of America, Inc.™
P.O. Box 19101, Washington, D.C. 20036

All rights reserved

Printed in the United States of America

ISBN: 0-8191-1051-5 (Perfect)

Library of Congress Number: 80-5124

TABLE OF CONTENTS

PREFACE

This study of middle-aged men using fictional literature as a data source was conducted in 1978 as a doctoral dissertation at Rutgers University. Interest in the study shown by graduate students and researchers in adult development and adult education has encouraged me to publish this work in its present form as prototype for subsequent investigations.

This study is unique in that grounded theory research was used in conjunction with fictional literature for studying one segment of adulthood--male middle age. Grounded theory is an inductive, theory building approach which emphasizes discovery rather than confirmation, hypothesis building rather than hypothesis testing. The detailed description of grounded theory research techniques offered in this study provides one of the few comprehensive descriptions available to investigators interested in employing grounded theory research methodology.

Using appropriate criteria, twelve 20th century American fictional works were selected for analysis. This study confirmed my belief that literature offers the potential for uncovering significant insights into the process of adult development and aging. My results demonstrate that fiction can indeed generate new knowledge about a period of adulthood, as well as corroborate findings from empirically-based research. It is my hope that this monograph will stimulate further research into adult development using grounded theory research techniques and fictional literature as a data source.

This study could not have been undertaken or completed without the continued guidance and encouragement of Gordon Darkenwald, Rutgers University. I am grateful for his invaluable

support. I would also like to thank Harold Beder,
Rutgers University, and Leon McKenzie, Indiana
University, for their advice and assistance in this
study.

January, 1980   Sharan B. Merriam

"Perhaps the most useful studies in the immediate future will...be those that depend upon inductive approaches and methods of naturalistic observation rather than upon deductive and experimental approaches."

-Bernice L. Neugarten

"And what indeed is literature but a record of human behavior?"

-Martin S. Lindauer

CHAPTER I

LITERATURE AND ADULT DEVELOPMENT

While educators have long recognized the
value of linking knowledge of child development
with the education of youth, little has been done
to correlate educational programming to the developmental processes of adults. At least two things
might explain this deficiency. First, there has
been comparatively little research done in the
area of adult development. It has been assumed
until recently that once a person reached adulthood, whether defined chronologically or socially,
one remained static until the dying process began.
Research within the last 25 years has shown that
adulthood is not one long unchanging plateau, but
that, in fact, patterns or stages of development
can be identified throughout adulthood. Secondly,
adult students have been seen as a homogeneous
group and taught by teachers using techniques
appropriate for primary and secondary students.
Historically, education has been used as a means
of preparing young people to assume the responsibilities of adulthood. Any learning past entry
into adulthood has been viewed as either filling
in gaps missed in traditional schooling, or
engaging in innocuous recreational activities.
Fortunately, this situation is also changing.
With an increase in the adult-aged population,
with a growing need for on-going training and
retraining, with more leisure time, adult education
is becoming increasingly visible as a discipline
having its own goals, methodology and programming.

Adult education and adult developmental
psychology are complementary fields of study. The
educational needs and interests of the adult to a
large extent reflect different stages of psycho-
social development. Understanding adult development can be an asset in planning adult educational
experiences. Birren and Woodruff (1973) suggest

1

that the goals of "educational intervention over the life span" are threefold: alleviation of educational deprivation; enrichment, to stimulate interest in learning itself; and prevention of difficulties in adjusting to different stages of the life span. With these goals in mind, an in-depth knowledge "of the developmental tasks facing adults at various age levels would appear to pro-vide a focus and a degree of relevancy to adult education" (p. 319). Knowledge and awareness of adult stages of life can thus provide a valuable resource for the adult educator in terms of diag-nosing learning needs and designing educational activities.

Indeed, a basic understanding of adult development is useful not just for the educator, but for anyone involved in helping adults to adjust, grow or change. According to Knox (1977, pp. 6-7), practitioners who familiarize themselves with knowledge of adult development will gain in-sight and perspective on their own lives as well as a better understanding of 1) the holistic or comprehensive character and coherence of an individual's adult life, 2) the interrelationship among generations, and 3) transitions adults make from one set of developmental tasks to another.

Traditional sources for developing life cycle paradigms are clinical practices, biogra-phies, surveys, and interviews. The relative recency of research in adulthood as well as the lack of clearly defined procedures for the study of adult development invites new and creative approaches to exploring the phases of adulthood.

Fictional literature would seem to be one rich source of data for acquiring knowledge about adult development. The link between literature and psychology has long been recognized:

And what indeed is <u>literature</u> but
a record of human behavior? And
just that is also the definition
given at the beginning of many a
discourse on the subject matter of
<u>psychology</u>....We interpret modern
literature...as being an attempt to
get at real facts which may throw
light upon human behavior.
(Lindauer, 1974, p. 67)

Literature has a lasting and universal appeal because
it speaks to the human condition. Whether literature
is approached as art and read for enjoyment, or as
knowledge and studied as a source of data, "the
writer discovers and communicates facts and their
meanings about human experience and behavior relevant to all men" (Lindauer, 1974, p. 82). Wellek
and Warren (1942), in a discussion of the various
functions of literature, note the value of literary
works to psychologists as source books or case
histories for when one considers the "very limited
number of persons whose inner life and motivations
we know"...it is "the great service of the novel
that it does reveal the introspective life of the
character" (p. 23).

        The potential usefulness of literature for
illuminating stages of adult development invites
systematic research. According to McKenzie (1975):

            Analysis of....literature can be a
            research modality for the simple
            reason that such research has the po-
            tential of making new information avail-
            able. A large number of creative
            artists have much to say about adult
            development and learning. What they
            have to say is based on their exper-
            ience, on exceptional perceptions of
            life, and on penetrating insights and
            profound intuitions. The author...offers
            to the researcher a conceptual model of
            human development. (pp. 214-215)

3

A desire to explore the usefulness of
literature as a data source for studying adult
development thus provided the impetus for this
research investigation. The various stages of
adulthood were considered in order to provide a
focus for the study. Out of the following stages
considered--young adulthood, middle age, old age,
death and dying--middle age was chosen for the
following reasons: 1) it was of most interest
to the researcher; 2) compared with the other
stages of adulthood, there has been less research
done on middle age; 3) middle-aged adults com-
prise a large, influential segment of the adult
population; implications for educational intervention based upon the study's findings could
thus have a potentially significant impact.

An initial exploration of the research on
middle age suggested a further limitation. Rather
than studying both sexes or women, middle-aged men
were chosen to be a focus of the study because:
1) the psychological literature suggests that
women follow different developmental patterns and
to include both males and females in the same
study would present problems of interpretation;
2) empirical research, which formed a reference
point for this study's findings, has focused
primarily on men, and 3) fictional literature
dealing with middle age has more often centered
on male rather than female protagonists.

With middle-aged males as the focus of the
study and literature as a data source, it was felt
necessary to establish parameters with regard to
the literary selections. To control for excessive
variability in terms of language and cultural
factors and to enhance the probability that findings would have relevant implications for contemporary adult educational programming, the study
was limited to twentieth century American literary
works. Within this framework literary works were
selected from two different historical periods--
post World War I and post World War II. This
provided a data base broad enough to insure that
findings would not be affected by particular con-
ceptions of literary art. Using works from two

4

different periods encompassing a fifty year time span also afforded the researcher an opportunity to determine whether characteristics of men in mid-life appear stable over time, or if there appeared to be historical differences in the dynamics of male middle age.

Traditionally, literature has been most often used as an illustrative device. Rigorous methodological investigations of literature have been limited to content analysis in which the goals have been to determine "the reading ease of prose, comparing stylistic factors, settling authorship disputes, and understanding literature's intentions and effects on an audience" (Lindauer, 1974, p. 58). In order to investigate the viability of using literature as a data source for social science inquiry, it was felt that a systematic research methodology should be employed. Grounded theory, a research methodology which emphasizes theory discovery rather than theory verification, seemed to be particularly suited to an attempt to generate new insights about a particular period of adult development. By using the rigorous data analysis techniques of grounded theory research, this study sought to go beyond past efforts which have largely employed unsystematic and impressionistic approaches to the analysis of literary materials, and to provide a prototype of a disciplined investigation of literature for the purpose of generating new knowledge and insights into one phase of adulthood.

Purpose of the Study

The general purpose of this study was to generate new knowledge and insight into the male mid-life period of development. This was undertaken through a comparative analysis of literary works using the inductive methodological techniques of grounded theory research. Specifically, this study had the following objectives:

1) to uncover new insights, theoretical constructs and hypotheses related to the male mid-life period of adult development and to interpret these elements of theory into a general explanatory paradigm;

2) to explore both the utility and validity of literature as a data source for generating new knowledge about psycho-social development;

3) to explore and demonstrate the efficacy of applying grounded theory data analysis techniques to literary materials for the purpose of generating theoretical constructs;

4) to identify implications for educational intervention for the middle-aged male segment of the adult population.

Literature As A Data Source

Literature has often been used to illustrate various psychological processes. One textbook, Psychology Through Literature (Shrodes, Van Gundy, & Husband, 1943), uses sample literary selections to illuminate such topics as emotional conflict, the learning process, dreams and the unconscious, neuroses and psychoses. Kimmel (1974), in a book on adult development, illustrates major ideas throughout his chapter on "Dying and Bereavement" with excerpts from a short story by Leo Tolstoy (The Death of Ivan Ilych). He also suggests in the Preface that his textbook could be used in conjunction with readings in fiction such as Death of a Salesman.

Aside from an illustrative function, literature has more recently been used as a tool for psychological counseling (Lesser, 1962; Menninger, 1937; McKinney, 1977). Called bibliotherapy, the technique involves using fiction as a catalyst in the counseling process: "fiction makes us as readers aware of our own needs." Furthermore, McKinney writes,

6

> it satisfies unconscious needs....
> It allays guilts and anxieties, and
> it is an indirect means of dealing
> with problems that we frequently shun.
> Fiction helps us to recognize the
> bad within us and yet accept our-
> selves. It often leaves us refreshed
> and restored, heals intrapsychic
> tension, and is integrating (McKinney,
> 1977, p. 551).

Use of literature to illustrate a stage of life has been most recently coupled with the growing interest in gerontology. In a recent issue of The Gerontologist, Sohngen (1977) categorizes 87 contemporary novels with regard to their usefulness for studying gerontology. She notes that literature can "stretch our personal knowledge of the human condition" and that students of gerontology can use literature to better understand the complexity of the aging experience (p. 72). Loughman (1977), in the same issue, focuses on novels of senescence. Other writers (Jacques, 1965; McMorrow, 1974; McLeish, 1976) have discussed middle ages characteristics with reference to literary works by Keats, Shakespeare, Baudelaire, Dante, Maugham, Hesse, Hemingway, Fitzgerald and Bellow. Compared to old age and adolescence, however, middle age has attracted little use of literature to illuminate its developmental characteristics.

On occasion literature has been linked to adult development paradigms. Ricciardelli (1973) applied Cumming and Henry's disengagement theory to King Lear: "Lear emerges as a credible old man whose life cycle traces a modal pattern: Activity-- differential--disengagement--total disengagement-- death (p. 148). Bye (1975) analyzed the novel Nobody Makes Me Cry in terms of Peck's seven psychological attributes related to personality and adjustment in middle age. And using the alternate art form of film, Erik Erikson (1976) applied his model of adult development to Dr. Borg in Bergman's "Wild Strawberries."

The search uncovered a few instances where
literature was approached inductively. Butler
(1971) used descriptions of aging by a diverse
group of authors to develop the positive rather
than the negative aspects of the declining years.
Plank (1968) extracted the motives for space
travel from science fiction and children's literature in conjunction with nonliterary sources.

A precedent for using literature as a
source for generating new insight about a period
of human development can be found in the early
writings of Sigmund Freud. In The Interpretation
of Dreams, first published in 1900, Freud develops
his theory of the Oedipus complex from an analysis
of Sophocles' Oedipus Rex and Shakespeare's
Hamlet. The power of Oedipus Rex· to move a modern
audience was due, he felt, not so much to the
destiny versus human will theme, but to the fact
that Oedipus' destiny

> might have been ours--because the
> oracle laid the same curse upon us
> before our birth as upon him. It
> is the fate of all of us, perhaps,
> to direct our first sexual impulse
> towards our mother and our first
> hatred and our first murderous wish
> against our father....Here is one
> in whom these primaeval wishes of
> our childhood have been fulfilled,
> and we shrink back from him with the
> whole force of the repression by
> which those wishes have since that
> time been held down within us.
> While the poet, as he unravels the
> past, brings to light the guilt of
> Oedipus, he is at the same time com-
> pelling us to recognize our own
> inner minds, in which those same
> impulses, though suppressed, are
> still to be found (Freud, 1961,
> pp. 262-263).

8

Freud interprets Hamlet as having "its roots in
the same soil as Oedipus Rex." The only difference between the two is that in Oedipus "the
child's wishful phantasy that underlies it is
brought into the open and realized as it would
be in a dream. In Hamlet it remains repressed;
and--just as in the case of a neurosis--we only
learn of its existence from its inhibiting con-
sequences" (Freud, 1961, p. 264). Thus, the
Oedipus complex, a seminal construct, developed
largely out of an exploration of literary works -
in an attempt, Freud said, "to interpret the
deepest layer of impulses in the mind of the
creative writer" (Freud, 1961, p. 266).

Besides reviewing the ways in which literature has been linked to developmental psychology,
this study also relates to previously published
work dealing with middle age. While there is no
doubt that middle age constitutes a period of
human development in which significant personality
changes take place, there is little agreement
"about when it occurs--or about what it is that
changes" (Troll, 1975, p. 64).

Major research on middle age has been
based on intensive case studies, biographic
analysis, interviews and field studies. There is
also a segment of the literature which can best
be categorized as theorizing. Some theories have
been based on clinical practice, autobiographies
or unsystematic observations of behavior. Finally,
there is a popularized, self-help version of
middle age and mid-life crisis literature which is
basically a restatement of earlier writings,
interspersed with the author's personal opinions.
Comprehensive reviews of the literature on middle
age can be found in several publications (Merriam,
1978; Knox, 1979). In addition, findings from
empirically-based research are compared in Chapter V
to the findings from this study in which literature
is used as a data source.

Some generalizations can be made with regard
to the research on middle age which are important

9

for this study. To begin with, much of the empirical research suffers from methodological problems which limit the generalizability of the findings. Very few studies are based on a random sample; most subjects are white, middle class, and frequently male. The research is predominantly cross-sectional in design and does not take into account possible cohort-generational differences. Comparing a middle-aged group with a younger or older cohort may reveal differences which are not a function of the age of the subjects, but rather of the historical, social, and cultural experiences of particular generations. Several theories of middle age have been generated from atypical samples culled from psychoanalytic and psychotherapeutic practices.

Nevertheless, the literature on middle age when considered in its entirety does lend support to the following generalizations:

1) there is a growing awareness of time--that one's existence is finite;
2) it is a period of introspection and self-analysis which is believed by some investigators to be critical in terms of future growth and development;
3) it is potentially the most powerful stage of life in terms of earning capacity, influence on other people and impact on society in general;
4) there are developmental tasks unique to this stage of adult development;
5) there is a tendency towards a male-female role reversal--that is, men become more affiliative and passive, women more aggressive and independent.

With regard to middle-aged males in particular, the research suggests that men tend to define themselves in terms of career or work patterns, whereas women are more affected by events in the family cycle. Moreover, men more than women are concerned with bodily decline and changes in physical appearance. Neugarten (1968b) found this to be described by men as "the most salient characteristic of middle age" (p. 96).

Middle age, as well as other periods of the adult life cycle, is a relatively new area of investigation. With only a few exceptions, all of the research and theorizing on middle age has been done within the last twenty years. No single methodological procedure has been established as the preferred approach to studying this segment of the adult population, and there are only a few theoretical frameworks from which concepts can be operationalized. A review of the literature on middle age suggests that there is much room for further exploration and theory building.

CHAPTER II

THE APPLICATION OF GROUNDED THEORY
RESEARCH TO LITERARY MATERIALS

Theoretical Framework

In this study, an inductive comparative
analysis of selected twentieth century American
literary works was undertaken to generate theoretical insights into the male mid-life period of
development. Grounded theory, a research methodology developed by sociologists Glaser and
Strauss (1967), provided the analytical framework
for the inquiry. This methodology emphasizes
inductively generating theory which is "grounded"
in the data, rather than testing theory or merely
describing empirical phenomena. Unlike the traditional natural science model of empirical
research which emphasizes verification, grounded
theory is primarily concerned with discovery.
Neugarten (1973) writes in support of such an
approach for studying adult development:

> Given the fact...that those of our
> studies in which age differences
> were clearest were those in which
> the dimensions of personality were
> inductively derived, perhaps the
> most useful studies in the immediate
> future will also be those that
> depend upon inductive approaches and
> methods of naturalistic observations
> rather than upon deductive and experi-
> mental approaches (pp. 326-327).

Theory, according to Glaser and Strauss
(1967), "is a strategy for handling data in research, providing modes of conceptualization for
describing and explaining" (p. 3). Theory should
provide a perspective on behavior and be useful
for guiding future research. In order to fulfill

13

this function of usefulness, a theory must be derived from the data which it purports to describe or explain. The theory will then "fit"--that is, the categories will be "readily (not forcibly) applicable to and indicated by the data under study." It will also "work"--that is, the categories will be "relevant to and be able to explain the behavior under study" (Glaser & Strauss, 1967, p. 3).

The aim of grounded theory, then, is to generate theory that both "fits" and "works." Emerging directly from the data source, the evidence itself can be used to illustrate elements of the theory. Thus, theory which has emerged from a data source is potentially more useful than theory which is the result of speculative thinking based on a prior assumption. An inductive approach to theory building also has more potential for realizing the predictive and explanatory functions of theory than a purely deductive approach. Logico-deductive research imposes a preconceived paradigm upon a data source and seeks verification. The constraints of the design can severely hamper the possibility of discovery. Furthermore, because of its necessarily narrow focus, this approach often limits exploration of the interrelationships of variables. The grounded theory researcher is interested in both verification of the emerging theory and description, but only as secondary objectives. In grounded theory, the researcher's primary concerns are discovery and explanation.

A conceptual scheme generated by grounded theory methods consists of several elements. A category is "a conceptual element of theory" and can stand by itself. Properties are aspects of the category which define or illuminate the category's meaning. Categories and properties are generated by the data and "have a life apart from the evidence that gave rise to them." Concepts, according to Glaser and Strauss (1967):

14

should be analytic--sufficiently
generalized to designate characteristics of concrete entities,
not the entities themselves.
They should be sensitizing--yield
a 'meaningful' picture, abetted by
apt illustrations that enable one
to grasp the reference in terms of
one's own experience. (pp. 38-39)

A skeletal theory emerges as categories
and properties are abstracted from the data and
then related through the tentative formulation
of hypotheses. In grounded theory research,
"hypotheses have at first the status of suggested,
not tested, relations among categories and their
properties, though they are verified as much as
possible in the course of research" (Glaser &
Strauss, 1967, p. 39).

The basic strategy in grounded theory
research is the constant comparative method of
data analysis. Categories, properties and
hypotheses emerge simultaneously throughout the
process of data collection, coding and analysis.
There is no prescribed moment when the researcher
stops one operation and begins another. Unlike
other research methodologies, analysis begins
immediately. The "researcher moves back and
forth between data and concepts emerging from the
data, to develop clues to the emerging theory and
focus for further collection of data" (Marsick,
n.d., p. 7).

The traditional uses of comparative analysis as a research technique are incorporated into
the grounded theory approach. Comparative analysis 1) checks the accuracy of evidence by constant
referral back to the "facts"; 2) helps establish
the generality of a fact; 3) specifies a concept;
4) helps to verify a theory as it emerges; and
5) generates theory, for in grounded theory comparative analysis "both subsumes and assumes
verifications and accurate descriptions, but only
to the extent that the latter are in the service

15

of generation" (Glaser & Strauss, 1967, p. 28).

The constant comparative method of qualitative analysis is the heart of grounded theory research. This technique can be applied to a variety of data sources. Glaser and Strauss argue that documentary materials--"letters, biographies, autobiographies, memoirs, speeches, novels and a multitude of nonfiction forms"--are potentially valuable for generating theory (1967, pp. 161, 163). Since theory building rather than verification or description is the aim of grounded theory research, an open and flexible use of data sources is necessary and appropriate. What is most important is the emergent theory's explanatory and predictive powers. The nature of the underlying data source is important, but not to the same degree as in traditional descriptive or hypothesis-testing inquiry. Thus, qualitative documentary materials or previously collected quantitative data are seen as legitimate sources of evidence in a grounded theory study.

That researchers need not limit themselves to traditional data sources when generating theory is further supported by an analysis of the "root sources of all significant theorizing." Theory, Glaser and Strauss postulate, comes in part from

> the sensitive insights of the
> observer himself. As everyone
> knows, these can come in the
> morning or at night, suddenly
> or with slow dawning, while at work
> or at play (even when asleep);
> furthermore, they can be derived
> directly from theory (one's own or
> someone else's) or occur without
> theory; and they can strike the ob-
> server while he is watching himself
> react as well as when he is observ-
> ing others in action. Also, his
> insights may appear just as fruit-
> fully near the end of a long inquiry
> as near the outset. (1967, p. 251)

Insights which lead to emerging theory can thus come from personal experiences as well as the experiences of others:

> The validity of this point is
> easy to grasp if one thinks of an
> interviewer beginning to theorize
> on the basis of insight gotten
> from an interviewee's words. The
> anthropologist also does this when
> he listens to informants. If we
> can do this with an interviewee or
> an informant, why not with the author
> of an autobiography or a novel?
> What is more, the insider (interviewee,
> informant, novelist) may not give us
> the insight unwittingly; he may
> offer it intentionally, fully aware
> that he is doing so. If the
> researcher accepts that offer at
> face value, there is no sound
> methodological reason why he cannot
> begin to build, or further build,
> theory upon it. (pp. 252-253)

The fact that literature as a data source resists the rigorously controlled manipulation of "harder" evidence does not preclude its value as a medium for research. Analysis of data, even that which is rigorously collected, suffers to some extent from conceptual and methodological shortcomings inherent in the particular research methodology employed. According to Lindauer (1974):

> Literature can be thought of as one
> of many sources of psychological in-
> formation which vary in their degree
> of rigor and comprehensiveness.
> Literature's problems as a source of
> data, arising because it is an histor-
> ical record of fiction by...authors
> who were more concerned with literary
> than scientific criteria, are balanced
> by its major advantage: it gives the

insibehts of talented people about
important problems. (p. 82)

The value of literature as a data source can be
evaluated "only in terms of its fruitfulness...in
light of the data, hypotheses and theories which
will eventually emerge (Lindauer, 1974, p. 177).

In assessing the credibility of theory
generated from literature or similar data sources,
other scholars must first be presented with a
clear explanation of how the researcher obtained
the theory from the data. A codified procedure
for analyzing data is essential; the constant
comparative techniques of grounded theory research
provide just such a rigorous procedure. The value
of the theory itself can then be determined by
applying the following criteria suggested by
Glaser and Strauss:

1) Fitness--a theory must fit the substantive area to which it will be applied; a theory
which is closely related to the reality of the
substantive area of investigation is one which has
been carefully inducted from the data;

2) Understanding--laypersons working in
the substantive area should be able to understand
and use the theory;

3) Generality--categories of the generated
theory "should not be so abstract as to lose their
sensitizing aspect, but yet must be abstract
enough to make...theory a general guide to multi-
conditional, everchanging daily situations"
(p. 242);

4) Control--a theory must provide understanding of enough concepts and their interrelationships "to enable the person who uses it to
have enough control in everyday situations to make
its application worthwhile" (1967, pp. 238-245).

In summary, this study, by applying grounded
theory methodological procedures to literary data

18

sources, attempted to discover new information and insights on a specific period of adult development. The substantive area of investigation was the psycho-social development of middle-aged men. Selected twentieth century works of American fiction provided the data source for generating theoretical constructs concerning the dynamics of male middle age.

Selection of Materials

Twentieth century American literature was used to develop theoretical insights into the male mid-life period of adulthood. It was judged that twelve literary works--six post World War I and six post World War II--would provide sufficient data to achieve the purposes of this study. More novels (four from each period) then plays (two from each period) were chosen because of the novel's greater potential for character development and analysis. Poetry, due to complexities of metaphorical interpretation, and autobiography, which is non-fiction and which often encompasses an entire life span, were two literary forms not included in this study.

The following criteria, suggested by McKenzie (1976), were used as guidelines in the selection of particular works: 1) that they possess literary merit. Speaking of this criterion Lindauer states:

> The classics, standard works, and
> other literary forms of acknowledged
> and sustained merit, as consistently
> judged by experts over time, are more
> likely to provide information on uni-
> versal and pervasive psychological
> processes and traits; and their validity
> is confirmed by continued and sustained
> acceptance from an informed reader-
> ship....The classics, unlike popular
> works and stories in the mass media,

are less likely to be limited by
the changing patterns of societal
events. (pp. 180-181)

2) that the works be relevant to the problem; 3)
that the works be sufficient in length to derive
adequate information; and 4) that the works be
clearly written and unhampered by complex symbolism.

The actual selection of specific works was
based on the writer's own literary judgement and
consultations with professors in the field of
American literature. Seven college and university
professors were asked to name fictional works of
literary merit from the post World War I and
post World War II eras in which the protagonist
was a middle-aged male. In addition, a professor
of drama whose specialization is post World War I
drama was consulted for suggestions from this
period. Those works which were repeatedly listed
as meeting the required criteria were selected
for the study. They are:

Post World War I Period

Novels:

Cather, Willa. The Professor's
House. (1925)
Fitzgerald, F. Scott. Tender is
the Night. (1934)
Lewis, Sinclair. Babbitt. (1922)
Wolfe, Thomas. You Can't Go Home
Again. (1940)

Plays:

Howard, Sidney. They Knew What
They Wanted. (1924)
Rice, Elmer. The Adding Machine.
(1923)

Post World War II Period

Novels:

Bellow, Saul, <u>Herzog.</u> (1964)
Heller, Joseph. <u>Something Happened</u>.
    (1975)
Marquand, John P. <u>Point of No</u>
    <u>Return</u>. (1949)
Updike, John. <u>A Month of Sundays</u>.
    (1975)

Plays:

Miller, Arthur. <u>Death of a Salesman</u>.
    (1949)
Williams, Tennessee. <u>The Night of</u>
    <u>the Iguana</u>. (1961)

The above works chosen for analysis meet
the pre-established selection criteria. The award
winning reputations of the authors and the critical
acclaim given the novels and plays satisfy the criterion of literary merit. Five authors--Sinclair
Lewis, Sidney Howard, Tennessee Williams, Arthur
Miller, and John P. Marquand--have received the
Pulitzer Prize for their works; two authors--
Sinclair Lewis and Saul Bellow--were awarded the
Nobel Prize in literature. Others have been recognized through the National Book Award, New York Drama
Critics Award, and various international literary
awards.

The second criterion, that the works be
relevant to the problem, was also met by the works
selected for this study. Each play and novel has
a middle-aged male as the main protagonist. The
plots revolve around the presence and actions of
a man in mid-life. As opposed to a poem or short
story, the works selected were also sufficiently
long enough to allow for character development,
thus providing adequate information for analysis.
Finally, in regard to the last criterion, all of
the works were relatively free of complex symbolism
or stylistic devices which might have interfered
with the analysis.

21

Analyzing the Data

The use of grounded theory as a methodological framework in a research investigation calls for a specific explanation of how the emergent theory was derived from the data. In this study, twelve fictional works were used to generate insights about middle-aged men. Data collection and analysis were preceded by a cursory reading of the works in order to familiarize the researcher with the basic setting, plot, and characters. A detailed reading of each work was then undertaken.

As the researcher moved through the first novel, The Professor's House, any incident, dialogue, or statement made or thought by the protagonist or other characters which appeared to relate to middle age was underlined. In using the grounded theory methodology, a researcher cannot help but to approach the data with at least sketchy ideas of what to look for. This provides a starting point for data collection. A strong attempt is made, however, to remain open and sensitive to what the data source might possibly generate. In The Professor's House, (Cather, 1925), for example, the first underlined item was a statement describing the professor's eyes--"They had lost none of their fire, though just now the man behind them was feeling a diminution of ardour" (p. 13). It was thought that a "diminution of ardour" might relate to a felt loss of vitality or energy associated with growing older. On a separate piece of paper, page number and "diminution of ardour" were recorded under the tentative heading "Aging." The next item underlined and recorded was a dialogue between the professor and Augusta, the family seamstress. They are discussing her long service and the fact that she has grown "grey." Godfrey St. Peter is disturbed by the remark. This interchange with page number was recorded under the tentative category "Awareness of Time." This procedure was followed through the book. Some fifty-two different page numbers and core quotes were noted under nine different categories such as appearance, mentor, wife, career.

After completing The Professor's House, a theoretical memo was typed in which the researcher noted generalities, ideas, strong themes having to do with being middle-aged which had emerged from the book.

This process of underlining and notetaking continued with the close reading of Babbitt, a difference being that the tentative categories generated by The Professor's House were kept in mind by the researcher. Although looking for some verification of these categories in Babbitt, new categories and re-focusing of earlier categories were also sought. Over one hundred page numbers and core quotes were recorded and two new categories, "Introspection" and "Burdened by Responsibility" emerged. Besides typing a lengthy memo recording thoughts on Babbitt, the researcher typed a memo recording joint observations pertaining to Babbitt and the Professor. The researcher noted such common experiences as an awareness of time, concern with physical aspects of aging and loss of interest in work. A note was also made that these two men's rebellions ended in resignation and acceptance, a movement similar to Kubler-Ross' theory (1969) on the acceptance of death.

With the reading of successive literary works, verification and strengthening of earlier categories was sought while at the same time an attempt was made to avoid forcing new data to fit preconceived categories. Rather, each work, to the extent possible, was allowed to generate its own categories or headings. Occasionally, a salient quote was recorded under two apparently appropriate headings. Tom Marshfield's feeling that it was too late to leave the ministry, for example, was noted under "Awareness of Aging" and "Career Concerns." A memo for each book, comparative memos, as well as an occasional theoretical memo were also typed. A particularly insightful remark by Dick Diver in Tender is the Night, for example, prompted a memo on the sense of fragmentation in middle age.

23

As works were compared and contrasted with one another, themes began to emerge into which the data could be divided. Quotes from the works fell into clusters with themes such as aging, family, work, and self. Each cluster of quotes was continually added to while at the same time analyzed by the researcher in an attempt to determine a pattern of categories and properties. Sifting through the quotes related to family relationships, for example, it was noticed that the protagonists were involved with their own generation, their parents and their children. This suggested the notion that family relationships for the middle-aged man centered around being the middle of two generations. The mid-generational position began to emerge as a possible category, that is, a general concept that could encompass the data found in the "family" cluster. The data was then looked at for its ability to explain what it meant to be mid-generation. It was found that the quotes could be further sub-divided into three areas: those in which the protagonist complained about being responsible for all three generations; those which expressed envy of the younger generation and fear of becoming like the older; and those that showed the men resenting parental pressure. These three subdivisions of data all connoted pressure upon a protagonist caught in the middle. The idea of being "squeezed" from both ends led to naming the category "generation squeeze." The three subdivisions then become properties of the category—that is, they served to define and illuminate the more general concept of generation squeeze.

Each cluster of quotes was analyzed in much the same manner. In the "generation squeeze" example, the category provided the conceptual element under which the properties were subsumed. In the following example, a set of quotes became a property which led, in turn, to the formulation of a category. Several of the protagonists assumed the role of mentor to a younger man. Mentorship was an early heading which was at first thought to be related to the career cluster. In seeking

24

to understand why a man might be a mentor, it was discovered that the mentorship quotes had less to do with career than with feeling young again through the presence of a mentee. Being a mentor was a rejuvenating, revitalizing activity. At this point all the data was reviewed for evidence of other ways in which the protagonists tried to feel young. Many of the men, for example, took on young lovers and/or increased their level of sexual activity. Quotes related to this phenomenon revealed that the men perceived sexual activity as a means of proving to themselves, at least temporarily, that they had the stamina of a younger man. Sexual exploits caused them to feel youthful. Sexual activity and mentoring were thus subsumed as properties of the category, ego rejuvenation.

As the relationships between categories and properties began to crystallize, earlier read works were returned to for verification. A few categories were eliminated as being unique to one or two men and/or not particularly sensitizing to middle age. Before they were dropped, specific incidents recorded in these categories were reviewed for their usefulness in explaining other concepts of middle age. The category "Unhappiness" was eliminated as not particularly revealing, but each incident was first reviewed with the researcher asking the question "unhappy about what?"

After all twelve works were read and data recorded in this manner, all notes, recorded data, comparative and theoretical memos were reviewed. Extracted from the data were five major categories and their properties deemed characteristic of the male mid-life period of development. These categories, properties, and the twelve literary works were each assigned a number which could then be punched on McBee Key Sort Cards.

At this point in the study a duplicate set of books was purchased. For each literary work, all underlined incidents in the original book were then cut out of the duplicate book and pasted on a McBee card. The card was punched according to

25

the coded categories and properties. This systematic coding of the data resulted in the researcher reviewing all incidents in all of the books. Even at this point in the study, categories and properties were continually analyzed with an eye to refining them so that they reflected the data as precisely as possible. In many instances, an episode or thought pasted on a card was punched for more than one category or property. This cross referencing generated thinking about the interrelatedness of the categories. Several tentative hypotheses emerged, as well as thoughts on the integration of the data into an overall theory of middle age. All such insights were recorded.

The analysis and writing of the findings of this study were greatly facilitated by having coded and stored all the data on McBee cards. By pulling all cards coded for a specific category or literary work, the researcher was given instant access to pertinent data. Analysis of categories continued through the writing of the findings. Upon pulling all cards coded for the property "reminiscence," for example, it was decided that reminiscence did not capture a quality of middle age so much as provide a mechanism for the author to relate background information on the protagonists.

In summary, from the reading of the first book through the writing of the findings, the researcher attempted to remain sensitive to what the data itself was generating about mid-life. The simultaneous collection and analysis of the data allowed for the emergence of categories and properties derived directly from the data. This cumulative process of theory building involved a simultaneous examination of evidence with the formulation of concepts and tentative hypotheses. Through the constant comparative method, each new piece of data served to confirm or modify elements of the emerging theory. The theory of middle age presented in this study has thus been developed through the techniques of grounded theory research.

CHAPTER III

MIDDLE AGE: THE ELEMENTS OF
AN INDUCTIVE THEORY

Childhood and adolescent development patterns have been well documented. The growth and development that occurs during adulthood is a relatively new area of investigation. The research which has been done, however, supports the contention that there are stages of development in the second half of life as well as the first half. It appears that each stage of life poses tasks to be mastered and issues to be grappled with. Continued growth and development depend, to a large extent, upon how well one handles the tasks unique to each stage. Young adults, the middle-aged and the elderly must all confront the issues salient to their segment of the life span. Researchers have investigated the nature of these issues and their interactive effects upon the adult with the goal of charting the process of adult development. In an effort to add to the understanding of one segment of the adult life span, this study focused on middle-aged males from twelve 20th century literary works.

Findings of this study suggest that coping with middle age can be an uncomfortable, and at times, painful endeavor. As with other stages of human development, the salient issues of mid-life must be met and successfully dealt with in order for there to be continued growth and development. In varying degrees, the lives of these twelve protagonists become fragmented as each pauses to scrutinize his career, his family, and himself. In some cases the protagonist realizes what is happening but is powerless to influence the process. Dick Diver in Tender is the Night (Fitzgerald, 1934) "tried to dissect it [life] into pieces small enough to store away--realizing that the totality of a life may be different in quality from its segments, and also that life during the

27

forties seemed capable of being observed only in segments" (Fitzgerald, 1934). Herzog (Bellow, 1964) struggles to "make a steady progress from disorder to harmony" (p. 255) and is "in pursuit of a grand synthesis" (p. 255). Indeed, this period of fragmentation in which the segments of one's life are analyzed, criticized and evaluated, is followed by a restructuring, putting the puzzle pieces of one's life back together. Restructuring, when it occurs, allows the middle-aged person to move on in life, to continue to grow and develop.

While the challenge of other stages of human development might also generate conflict necessitating a resolution, middle age can be differentiated from other life stages by its own distinctive psycho-social events. Fragmentation-restructuring is a broad conceptual framework within which the dynamics of middle age can be viewed. Fragmentation is best thought of as a continuum. Some protagonists experience intense distress and conflict as they attempt to cope with middle age; for others the process is less traumatic. Common to all protagonists, however, are the issues of mid-life which must be confronted. In this study, five major categories descriptive of middle age emerged from a comparative analysis of the data. It is the purpose of this chapter to explore the following mid-life categories and their properties: (1) awareness of aging, (2) search for meaning, (3) generation squeeze, (4) career malaise, and (5) ego rejuvenation.

Awareness of Aging

The data from this study strongly affirm that a growing awareness of one's own aging is a major concern for those in mid-life. Unlike a young person who is future oriented, whose life stretches ahead almost indefinitely, the middle-aged man begins to realize that his life is finite. He becomes aware of his physical aging, an irreversible process, which, he realizes, leaves him

left with a limited number of years. This awareness of aging is more fully understood by explaining its properties of a reordered time perspective,
concern with physical deterioration, intimations
of mortality, and peer/spouse confirmation.

The awareness of aging is characterized by
a reordered time perspective. The men in this
study begin to view their lives in terms of the
time they have left to live, rather than the number of years since birth. Bob Slocum in Something
Happened (Heller, 1975) graphically describes this
shift in time perspective with an analysis of his
sleeping position:

> In my middle years, I have ex-
> changed the position of the fetus
> for the position of a corpse.
> When I go to sleep now, it is no
> longer on my side with my knees
> tucked up securely against my
> abdomen, and my thumb near my
> mouth. I lie on my back with my
> hands clapped across my chest
> decorously like a cadaver and my
> face pointed straight up toward
> the ceiling. (p. 318)

Slocum wonders "how many years' worth of Sundays
do I have left: Thirty? Two?" (p. 477). He
decides he's "too old" and it's "too late" to
think about a divorce (p. 355). The shift in time
perspective finds expression in thinking about
his job:

> My job? When I am fifty-five, I
> will have nothing more to look
> forward to than Arthur Baron's
> job and reaching sixty-five.
> When I am sixty-five, I will have
> nothing more to look forward to
> than reaching seventy-five, or dying
> before then. And when I am seventy-
> five, I will have nothing more to
> look forward to than dying before
> eighty-five. (p. 523)

Other protagonists experience a realization of a reordered time perspective in different ways. Dick Diver (Fitzgerald, 1934) realizes that he "had been going through that partitioning of the things of youth wherein it is decided whether or not to die for what one no longer believes," (p. 133) and, as he leaves the Riviera realizes that "he was not young anymore" (p. 311). Godfrey St. Peter, the professor in The Professor's House (Cather, 1925), tries to pinpoint when the shift in time perspective took place but can only determine that his youth is gone and that he is a different person (p. 282). That the professor has shifted his time perspective is evidenced by the response to his wife who feels he should take better care of his health. "Why so?' he responds. 'It's not worth half so much as it was then.'" (p. 97). The minister in A Month of Sundays (Updike, 1975) measures time by the yardstick of adultery at different ages. Middle age, of which he realizes he is an example, is the period when "marriages are extended by surrender. The race between freedom and exhaustion is decided" (p. 164).

For Webber (Wolfe, 1940), a reordered time perspective comes on gradually. Webber says "It came in on me little by little, almost without my knowing it" (p. 560). He experiences a shift away from "the personal and self-centered vision of the world which a young man always has" (p. 561) to gradually discovering "a larger world outside" (p. 560). That this process is dependent upon aging and thus maturational is suggested by George's question, "Does one ever really learn from others till one is ready for the lesson?" (p. 562).

The shift in time perspective is a gradual process for Moses Herzog (Bellow, 1964), also. He says: "Maybe...I am going through a change of outlook" (p. 233). Recalling his mother's death he realizes that "He was one of the mature generation now, and life was his to do something with, if he could" (p. 46). Just as George Webber sees youth as self-indulgences, Herzog (Bellow, 1964) speaks of his youth as a "life of innocent sloth" and that in middle age "a Faustian spirit of discontent...descends on you (Bellow, 1964). He feels unable to cope with a second divorce at this "time of life" (p. 104).

With a shift in time perspective comes a concern with physical deterioration. Both real signs of physical aging and projected future physical problems heighten the protagonists' awareness of aging. Babbitt (Lewis, 1922) is concerned with his diet, his digestive system and the ill effects of smoking (p. 79). Looking through journal advertisements, he becomes "interested in a preparation which 'takes the place of exercise for sedentary men by building up depleted nerve tissue, nourishing the brain and the digestive system'" (p. 173).

Herzog goes shopping for new clothes being sure to check the ads in The New Yorker and Esquire because they "showed older men with lined faces as well as young executives and athletes" (p. 29). He is leary of new styles which make "middle-aged or paunchy old men" look "ludicrous" (p. 29). Besides feeling he has mismanaged his life, Herzog is disturbed that "he was losing his hair. He read the ads of the Thomas scalp specialists, with the exaggerated skepticism of a man whose craving to believe was deep, desperate" (p. 10). Herzog notes that keeping his country home in shape has "made his arms muscular. Extended the lease of narcissism a little while" (p. 191). Undressing for a physical exam, Herzog checks himself in the process of self-admiration: "He feared being caught in the part of the aging, conceited handsome man. Old fool, he called himself, glancing away from the small mirror, the graying hair, the wrinkles of amusement and bitterness" (p. 21). He is vaguely dissatisfied with the doctor's report that he is healthy--"not twenty-one, but strong" (Bellow, 1964, p. 21).

Bob Slocum in Something Happened (Heller, 1975) worries about his future deterioration with

a foreboding equal to his present concern with the
physical. "Everything feels old" (Heller, 1975,
p. 109) he complains. "How will I look when I'm
eighty and toothless....How will I smell" (p. 434).
"Maybe I'm senile already and people are too
kind to tell me" (p. 472). He feels he is moving
towards a fulfillment of all the ills of old age:

> I am growing forgetful. My eye-
> sight is deteriorating. I wear
> reading glasses now and require a
> stronger prescription every year.
> Periodontal work will save my teeth
> only for a while. I know I repeat
> myself at home with my children and
> my wife....Soon I'll be repeating
> myself with everyone everywhere and
> be shunned as a prattling old fool.
> (p. 402)

Slocum feels he is "in a headlong race toward
decrepitude" (p. 424). He notices that he has
"gotten a little paunchy and carries a sack
beneath [his] jaw" (p. 338).

Tom Marshfield in A Month of Sundays
(Updike, 1975) becomes very aware of his aging
body. "My digestion is perversely good," he
notes, "and my other internal units function with
the smoothness of subversive cell meetings in a
country without a government....My appendix is un-
excised. I feel it, and my heart, as time bombs"
(pp. 13-14). Looking at a snapshot of himself
taken by a fellow clergyman, Tom becomes acutely
aware of his stage in life:

> I see, not quite in focus, a middle-
> aged, quasi-mesomorphic clergyman
> doing an ungainly but solemn imitation
> of an athlete, beneath an alien desert
> sun, amid the trappings of vacation,
> in a moment innocuous and lost. I
> want to laugh, but my throat locks,
> dried by the realization that this is
> a picture of me in Paradise. (p. 230)

Willy Loman in Death of a Salesman
(Miller, 1949) wants to be taken off the road for,
he explains to his boss, "I'm just a little tired"
(p. 79). He tries to rationalize his lack of
success with age-related complaints: "I talk too
much"; "I joke too much!"; "I'm fat. I'm very
foolish to look at, Linda"' "I gotta overcome it.
I know I gotta overcome it. I'm not dressing to
advantage, maybe" (p. 37).

The protagonist of Point of No Return
(Marquand, 1949) also worries about how he looks.
His wife wants him to wear his gold service emblem. "The emblem placed him in a youthful category to which he did not belong. He was not sure
how well it looked at the bank, either" (p. 411).
Zero in The Adding Machine (Rice, 1923) realizes
his age as he becomes winded after dancing for a
few moments (p. 56). And Tony, the older man in
They Knew What They Wanted (Howard, 1924), sensitive to the fact that he is marrying a younger
woman, brags to all his ability to father children
until he's "one hundra year" sic old" (p. 141).

Concern with physical deterioration as
part of a growing awareness of age is confirmed by
spouses and/or peers. The men are either confronted with their aging by spouse/peer comments,
or they notice aging as it is occurring in others.

Augusta, the seamstress in The Professor's
House (Cather, 1925), tells Godfrey "when I first
came to sew for Mrs. St. Peter, I never thought I
should grow grey in her service" (p. 23). This
remark "amazed" and "troubled" Godfrey. Godfrey's
wife also acts as a sounding board for his own
aging:

> 'My dear,' he sighed when the
> lights were turned on and they
> both looked older, 'it's been a
> mistake, our having a family and
> writing histories and getting
> middle-aged. We should have been
> picturesquely ship-wrecked together
> when we were young.' (p. 94)

They accuse each other of growing more intolerant
(Cather, 1925, p. 35) and irritable (97). And in
a particularly revealing interchange Godfrey's
wife asks him why he has withdrawn from the family.
"'You are not old enough for the pose you take' she
says. "'For many years you never seemed to grow
at all older....Something has come over you.'"
(pp. 162-163). He replies that

> 'I can't altogether tell myself,
> Lillian. It's not wholly a matter
> of the calendar. It's the feeling
> that I've put a great deal behind me,
> where I can't go back to it again--
> and I don't really wish to go back....
> And now I seem to be tremendously
> tired. One pays, coming or going. A
> man has got only just so much in
> him; when it's gone he slumps.
> (p. 163)

Godfrey also notices how much his wife enjoys the
attentions of her sons-in-law. "She had begun
the game of being a woman all over again....She
wasn't going to have to face a stretch of boredom
between being a young woman and being a young
grandmother" (p. 79).

Babbitt (Lewis, 1922) sees in his wife a
reflection of his own aging. She was "definitely
mature" and in her full matronliness she was "as
sexless as an anemic nun" (p. 10). He finds her
dull and inhibiting and accuses her of doing her
"level best" to make him "old" (p. 295). Babbitt
views his neighbors in terms of their ages, also.
He decides that

> The difference between a light man
> like Sam Doppelbrau and a really fine
> character like Littlefield was revealed
> in their appearances. Doppelbrau
> was disturbingly young for a man of
> forty-eight....But Littlefield was old
> for a man of forty-two. (pp. 24-25)

But it is Babbitt's close friend Paul who does the most to nudge Babbitt into a middle-age rebellion. Paul is bored with his job, and unhappily married. He tells Babbitt that if one looked into the heads of their male friends he'd find "one-third of 'em are sure enough satisfied with their wives and kids and friends and their offices; and one-third feel kind of restless but won't admit it; and one-third are miserable and know it" (Lewis, 1922, p. 55). This happens, Paul says, at about "forty to forty-five....Why do you suppose there's so many mysterious suicides?" (p. 55). When Babbitt finally does rebel and have an affair, he vacillates between feeling elated and seeing his mistress as she really was:

> And he saw her now as middle-aged,
> as beginning to be old....She was
> old, he winced. Old! He noted
> how the soft flesh was creasing into
> webby folds beneath her chin, below
> her eyes, at the base of her wrists.
> A patch of her throat had a minute
> roughness like the crumbs from a
> rubber eraser. Old! (p. 293)

The protagonist in You Can't Go Home Again (Wolfe, 1940) also sees his lover as middle-aged-- "her face bore the markings of middle-age....When she was at work...she looked the oldest. It was then that one noticed the somewhat fatigued and minutely wrinkled spaces around her eyes and some strands of grey that were beginning to sprinkle her dark-brown hair" (p. 132). George sees his best friend Randy at intervals throughout the novel. At each encounter George is reminded of the aging process:

> But now something caught in George's
> throat as he looked at him and saw what
> time had done. Randy's lean, thin
> face was deeply furrowed, and the
> years had left a grey deposit at
> his temples. His hair was thinning
> back on both sides of the forehead,

and there were little webbings of
fine wrinkles at the corners of the
eyes. It saddened George and
somehow made him feel a bit ashamed
to see how old and worn he looked.
(Wolfe, 1940, p. 77)

Besides fearing that his wife's health will
"degenerate" before his own, thus adding an extra
burden to his life (Heller, 1975, p. 423), Bob
Slocum in Something Happened fears facing "the deterioration of any human being who has ever been
dear...even of chance acquaintance, or total
stranger" (p. 74). He is morbidly fascinated by
death or tragedy occurring to men his age. "Men
my age," he notes, "are starting to die of cancers,
strokes, and heart attacks" (p. 323). He's relieved
to find out that the man who fell dead in the
office building lobby was "too old to be me" (p.
474).

Other protagonists deal with the peer/
spouse confirmation of their own aging in various
ways. Charles Grey in Point of No Return
(Marquand, 1945) has trouble recalling the name of
a friend "eight or nine years older than he" because
"fifty is a period in life when time begins alter-
ing faces in all sorts of disagreeable and incon-
gruous ways" (p. 434). The minister in A Month of
Sundays (Updike, 1975) gives advice to his middle-
aged counselees which he himself could use - "she
is, and you must know this, at a stage in her
life where she should become reacquainted with
her own needs, after all these years of other-
directed activity" (p. 208). In a discussion with
his wife about having an affair, she asks "'What
brings this on, anyway?'" Tom fails to see the
irony of his response - "'Oh nothing, Middle Age.
Angst'" (p. 83). Finally the problems of Shannon,
the defrocked clergyman in The Night of the Iguana
(Williams, 1961), are compounded by the middle-aged
earthy Maxine, and the presence of the aged, fail-
ing old poet Nonno.

The awareness of aging is also characterized by intimations of mortality. The realization that one's existence is finite occurs in
conjunction with a reordered time perspective. No
longer does the future spread out indefinitely
before the protagonists as it did in young adulthood. Some men fear death, some accept it, and
others vow to fight it. But for all the men,
there is no escaping the awareness of its reality.

George Webber (Wolfe, 1940) becomes aware
of the finiteness of life at his aunt's funeral.
"It was an aching pity for himself and for all
men living, and in it was the knowledge of the
briefness of man's days, and the smallness of his
life, and the certain dark that comes too swiftly
and that has no end" (p. 8). In several other
instances (Willy Loman, Bob Slocum, Moses Herzog),
the death of a parent propels the protagonist into
the position of the oldest of the family clan and
consequently the one nearest death. Also, as one
ages, one's contemporaries are more likely to die.
Charles Grey (Marquand, 1949) muses over the death
of his friend: "The cleared desk still gave
Charles a curious feeling of incompleteness and a
mixed sense of personal pain and loss because he
had been more friendly with Arthur Slade than
with anyone else in the Stuyvesant--but then you
had to die sometime" (p. 427).

Herzog (Bellow, 1964), the humanist,
decides that "what makes us human...is our knowledge of death....For knowledge of death makes us
wish to extend our lives at the expense of others,
and this is the root of the struggle for power"
(p. 201). Understanding this does not make it
any easier for Herzog to face his own mortality.
When Herzog's lawyer suggests an insurance policy
to cover his child, Herzog asks indignantly "'What
makes you so sure I'll die first,'" (p. 110) and
tries to end the discussion quickly--"'Just now I
don't feel like making arrangements for my death'"
(p. 111). And in an imaginary conversation with
his mother, Herzog says "I have sometimes wished
it [death] would hurry up, longed for it to come

soon. But I am still on the same side of eternity as ever. It's just as well, for I have certain things still to do" (p. 397). That part of his mid-life crisis involves facing death is revealed in Herzog's discussion with an old friend:

> 'Have you read the book by that
> Hungarian woman Tina Zolkoly about
> what to do in 'these crises?'
> 'No, what does she say?'
> 'She prescribes certain exercises.'
> Moses was interested. 'What are they?'
> 'The main one is facing your own
> death.' (p. 329)

Bob Slocum in Something Happened (Heller, 1975) tries to avoid dealing with death. "Sudden death," he confesses, "still shakes me up, particularly when it strikes somebody who has always been in robust health" (p. 79). He refuses to relate to anyone "in whom I begin to perceive the first signs of irreversible physical decay and approaching infirmity and death....They become dead records in my filing system" (p. 95). He is not successful at avoiding thoughts of death and finally admits "I think about it all the time. I dwell on it. I dread it. I don't really like it" (p. 321). Slocum cannot come to terms with his own finiteness. He expects to battle to the end:

> I will not want to go. They will
> have to drag me down writhing and
> moaning, I like to think now, while
> I fight with mind, eyes, ears, to
> remain, but I know I will probably
> be undermined also by a liver or two
> kidneys while I'm concentrating all
> my forces on top, and I will give up
> the ghost without sensing I am doing
> so...I don't ever want to go. I
> hope I outlive everyone, even my
> children, my wife, and the Rocky
> Mountains. (p. 306)

38

As a Christian minister, Tom Marshfield (Updike, 1975) is responsible for interpreting death to his congregation. But he himself has problems with it. A "doubting Thomas" (p. 8), Marshfield confesses that "the end is not clear" (p. 240) that "I can't believe the world will go on spinning without me" (p. 221). He feels the added burden of being a clergyman who must "stand as steeples stand, as emblems; it is our station to be visible and to provide men with the opportunity to profess the impossible that makes their lives possible" (p. 249). Questioning the Christian belief that death leads to a glorious afterlife, Tom decides that "the only life we desire is this one" and

> all those who offer instead some
> gaseous survival of a personal essence,
> or one's perpetuation through children
> or good deeds or masterworks of art,
> or identification with the race of
> Man, or the blessedness of final and
> absolute rest, are tempters and
> betrayers of the Lord. (p. 248)

Unlike Slocum and Marshfield, Godfrey St. Peter (Cather, 1925) accepts death:

> He could remember a time when the
> loneliness of death had terrified
> him, when the idea of it was insup-
> portable. He used to feel that if
> his wife could but lie in the same
> coffin with him, his body would not be
> so insensible that the nearness of
> hers would not give it comfort. But
> now he thought of eternal solitude
> with gratefulness; as a release
> from every obligation, from every
> form of effort. It was the Truth.
> (p. 272)

Thus, whether the men accept, fear, or deny death as part of the aging process, middle age appears to be a time when one realizes the

finiteness of one's own life. A reordered time
perspective, concern with physical deterioration
and peer/spouse confirmation of the aging process
are all salient properties of middle-aged man's
awareness of aging.

Search for Meaning

Coming to grips with one's aging is a major
task of middle age. The realization that one is
half way through life also catapults the protagonists into a search for meaning, a second category
uncovered in this study. Everything in the protagonists' lives comes under review. Unlike an
adolescent who is struggling to forge an identity,
a man in mid-life wonders who he has become.
Identifying anchors of family, career and self no
longer seem relevant. The returns on an invest-
ment of forty or so years of living are found to
be elusive. One property characteristic of the
mid-life search for meaning is an intense questioning of life in general and one's own life in
particular. The questioning of life leads the
men into feeling that they are losing their bearings, the second property of the search for meaning
category.

For the middle-aged male, the questioning
of life, which is descriptive of the search for
meaning, often encompasses a review of one's
earlier years. Godfrey St. Peter (Cather, 1924)
looks back on his boyhood and decides that it was
the "realest of his lives" and that "his career,
his wife, his family, were not his life at all,
but a chain of events which had happened to him.
All these things had nothing to do with the person
he was in the beginning" (p. 264). At another
time he sat at his desk "reviewing his life, trying to see where he had made his mistake, to
account for the fact that he now wanted to run
away from everything he had intensely cared for"
(p. 275). Dick Diver (Fitzgerald, 1934) questions
who he is and muses that perhaps "for the remainder
of his life he was condemned to carry with him the

egos of certain people...and to be only as complete
as they were complete themselves" (p. 245).
Babbitt (Lewis, 1922) moves from complacency to
restless boredom in which he had "doubts regarding life and families and business" (p. 17) to a
rebellion which he little understands:

> Why, he wondered, would he be in
> rebellion? What was it all about?
> 'Why not be sensible; stop all this
> idiotic running around, and enjoy
> himself with his family, his busi-
> ness, the fellows at the club?'
> What was he getting out of rebellion?
> Misery and shame--...'And yet.'
> Whatever the misery, he could not
> regain contentment with a world
> which, once doubted, became absurd.
> (p. 236)

As a writer, George Webber (Wolfe, 1940)
is particularly sensitive to the people and the
world around him. He questions his youthful "in-
satiable urge to know everything" which caused
him to feel he was "drowning in some vast sea of
his own sensations and impressions." Growing up,
he decided, means gaining a "perspective and de-
tachment" (pp. 429-430). Nevertheless, man who
"makes histories...and directs the destiny of
nations...does not know his own history, and he
cannot direct his own destiny with dignity or
wisdom for ten consecutive minutes" (p. 337).

Charles Grey in Point of No Return
(Marquand, 1949), less introspective than some of
the other protagonists, feels most uncomfortable
when a friend asks, "'Don't you ever get to won-
dering what everything's about?...Do you ever
wonder whether everything is worth while?'" (p. 451).
Willy Loman (Miller, 1949), who has trouble facing
the reality of his situation, even exclaims at one
point, "all of a sudden everything falls to pieces!"
(p. 66).

41

The questioning of the meaning of one's life is an identity crisis--not like that of the adolescent who wonders who he is becoming--but of men in mid-life who wonder who they have become. Moses Herzog (Bellow, 1964) says, "There is someone inside me. I am in his grip. When I speak of him I feel him in my head, pounding for order. He will ruin me" (p. 19). At another point he asks "Where is that human life which is my only excuse for surviving! What have I to show for myself?...My God! Who is this creature?" (p. 270). "Is there nothing else between life and death but what I can get out of this perversity--only a favorable balance of disorderly emotions? No freedom?" (p. 254).

Tom Marshfield in A Month of Sundays (Updike, 1975) asks himself "Who am I" (p. 11) and seeing his face in the mirror, says, "I do not recognize it as mine. It no more fits my inner light that the shade of a bridge lamp fits its bulb" (p. 7). Bob Slocum (Heller, 1975) is equally puzzled. Finding it easy to copy others' behavior, he wonders what his own true nature is and finally admits to himself, "I don't know who or what I really am" (p. 65). At another point Slocum rationalizes "There is no one else I would rather be than me even though I don't really like me and am not even sure who it is I am" (p. 163). He feels that he "never became what he wanted to be" (p. 319) even though he cannot articulate what he wanted to be. And pondering on his name he says, "I am not Bob Slocum just because my parents decided to call me that. If there is such a person, I don't know who he is" (Heller, 1975, p. 461).

The intense questioning of all things in their lives which had formerly given meaning to their existence results in the protagonists feeling a loss of bearings. This second property of the search for meaning varies in intensity from a feeling of drifting puzzlement to a fear of losing touch with reality.

42

Babbitt (Lewis, 1922) begins to "drift away" (p. 290) from his family and his real estate business. He tries to keep "himself from the bewilderment of thinking" (p. 218). "He was restless. He vaguely wanted something more diverting than the newspaper comic strips" (p. 219). A "curst discontent" tortures him, (p. 107) he feels "vaguely frightened" (p. 254) and yearns for the security of the way things used to be (p. 255). He finds little comfort in his rebellion--having an affair, drinking and dancing with a racy crowd only momentarily relieves his discontent. His foray into a life of carousing fails to provide the anchors he so desperately seeks. "Before long he admitted that he would like to fly back to the security of conformity" (p. 301).

St. Peter in The Professor's House (Cather, 1925) expresses the loss of bearings as a "falling out." "Falling out, for him, seemed to mean falling out of all domestic and social relations, out of his place in the human family" (p. 275). He has lost what he feels "makes men happy, believing in the mystery and importance of their own little individual lives" (p. 68). By "falling out" he is able to dispassionately view his own life: "He did not regret his life, but he was indifferent to it. It seemed to him like the life of another person" (p. 267). Loss of bearings for Godfrey St. Peter is akin to floating. "The university, his new house, his old house, everything around him, seemed insupportable, as the boat in which he is imprisoned seemed to a seasick man" (p. 150).

For Slocum (Heller, 1975) the sensation of "floating" is strong:

> I feel afloat (legless). Legless, I walk around with headaches that do not seem to be mine....I do not always feel securely connected to my legs or to my own past....Mountainous segments of my history appear to be missing...I do not always know where I am at present. (pp. 471-472)

43

"I keep my own counsel," Slocum says, "and drift
speechlessly with my crowd. I float" (p. 286).
Slocum fears he is losing control in his search
for meaning: "There are things going on inside
me," he says, "I cannot control and do not
admire" (p. 121):

> And I sometimes think I am losing my
> mind. The fear (and the mind I am
> losing) does not even seem to be
> mine...broiling in my insides one
> moment like a blast furnace, chilling
> my whole skin like foggy winter wind
> the next. Alternating out of control
> against me from within and without."
> (p. 389)

Slocum asks "Am I demented already, in...the
prime of my life?" (p. 474). Paralyzed by his own
brooding, Slocum has lost his power to "upset
things"--and an "act of rebellion would be absorbed
like rain on an ocean and leave no trace" (p. 15).

Like Slocum who feels "disoriented" in
both his "inner" and "outer world" (p. 227),
Shannon in The Night of the Iguana (Williams, 1961)
tells Hannah that he lives on two levels--"the
realistic level and the fantastic level" and
cannot tell "which is the real one" (p. 74). He
too, has lost his bearings. Hannah tells him his
problem is the "oldest one in the world--the need
to believe in something or in someone" (p. 106).

As Dick Diver (Fitzgerald, 1934) tries to
find meaning in his life, he is overcome by feelings of being lost, by doubts about himself. "I'm
not much like myself any more," (Fitzgerald, 1934,
p. 256) he says. Overhearing a prayerful chant by
two men, Dick "let them pray for him too, but what
for, save that he should not lose himself in his
increasing melancholy" (p. 256). Herzog's
(Bellow, 1963) search for meaning is also melancholy.
He tells himself he should "continue his studies,
aiming at the meaning of life" (p. 229). In his
search, he writes, "I temporarily lost my bearings"

(Bellow, 1963, p. 62). He no longer feels the
"stone-like certitude of archaic man" but rather
feels "his own individual character cut off at
times both from facts and values" (p. 134). He
too, worries whether he has crossed the fine line
into insanity. He gets a list of traits of para-
noia from a psychiatrist (p. 99); he writes
letters which are never sent and wonders if this
might be a symptom of disintegration (p. 10).

Charles Grey (Marquand, 1949) and George
Webber (Wolfe, 1940) are two protagonists who cope
more easily with their search for meaning. For
Grey, the distress is not much more than having a
cold:

> All he could do was to recognize
> his present state of mind as a def-
> inite malady like a cold or a fever
> and tell himself that it would pass.
> First there was a period of general
> uneasiness about nothing in particu-
> lar, than a growing illusion of being
> hemmed in, followed by a desire to
> escape, and finally an indescribable
> sense of loneliness mingled with a
> sort of self-pity which he particu-
> larly hated. (p. 504)

Webber finds the restlessness, the uncer-
tainty of his search for meaning to be what life
is all about:

> the essence of belief is doubt, the
> essence of reality is questioning.
> The essence of Time is Flow not Fix.
> The essence of faith is the knowledge
> that all flows and that everything
> must change. The growing man is
> Man-Alive, and his 'philosophy' must
> grow, must flow, with him. (p. 566)

In conclusion, the data from this study
suggest that middle age men become engaged in a
search for meaning. Midway through life they

evaluate who they have become and the factors in
their lives which have provided a basis for self
identity. A questioning of life and a loss of
bearings were properties descriptive of the search
for meaning.

The Generation Squeeze

The fragmentation each protagonist experiences as he attempts to cope with middle age is
exacerbated by the problems associated with being
the middle of three generations. Unlike a young
person who is responsible to an older generation,
or an elderly person who nurtures a younger generation, the middle-aged man is responsible to the
younger and the older generation. As Tom
Marshfield aptly expresses in A Month of Sundays
(Updike, 1975): "Heredity...worked up as well as
down" (p. 145).

Weaving in and out of the labyrinth of
intimate relationships to spouse, parents and
children, the mid-life male feels burdened by
having to offer emotional succor and financial
support to more people than at any other stage of
life. The protagonists feel "squeezed" from both
ends of the life span. Being responsible for
both the older generation, their parents, and
the younger generation, their children, is a
burden most would like to escape. Thus the property of oppressive responsibility helps to illuminate
the nature of the category generation squeeze.

Babbitt (Lewis, 1922) feels oppressed by
the responsibility he feels towards his children,
parents and wife. "'I'm sick of it!'" He rages...

> Having to carry three generations.
> Whole damn bunch lean on me. Pay
> half of mother's income, listen to
> Henry T., listen to Myre's worrying,
> be polite to Mart, and get called
> an old grouch for trying to help the
> children. All of 'em depending on

46

me and picking on me and not a damn
one of 'em grateful! No relief, and
no credit, and no help from anybody.
And to keep it up for--good Lord,
how long?' (Lewis, 1922, p. 190)

When he falls sick and is home from work he confesses to having "enjoyed" it; "he was delighted
by their consternation that he, the rock, should
give way" (p. 190). Babbitt's (Lewis, 1922)
desire to escape his responsibilities grows
stronger as he grows more aware of his aging.
Contemplating a vacation with his friend Paul,
he says, "'I'd like to get away from--everything'"
(p. 104). He unhappily realizes that the family's
high standard of living necessitates his being a
slave to his work: "He sulkily admitted now that
there was no more escape, but he lay and detested
the grind of the real-estate business, and disliked
his family, and disliked himself for disliking
them" (p. 7). On a therapeutic vacation trip to
the backwoods of Maine, he toys with the idea of
never returning. "There'd be enough money at home
for the family to live on till Verona was married
and Ted self-supporting" he rationalizes. "Why
not? Really live" he asks.

He longed for it, admitted that
he longed for it, then almost believed
that he was going to do it. When-
ever common sense snorted, 'Nonsense!
Folks don't run away from decent
families and partners: just simply
don't do it, that's all!' (p. 238)

Even when he rebels and has an affair Babbitt
cannot escape the pressures of his position. He
says to his mistress, "'Well, I'm not much. But
by golly I begin to feel middle-aged sometimes;
all these responsibilities and all'" (p. 260).

The responsibilities of parenthood are
particularly trying for many of the protagonists.
After a family breakfast marred by arguing, Babbitt
says "'I simply can't stand it....After a man's

spent his lifetime trying to give his kids a
chance and a decent education, it's pretty dis-
couraging to hear them all the time scrapping
like a bunch of hyenas'" (Lewis, 1922, p. 20).
Tom Marshfield in A Month of Sundays (Updike,
1975) feels trapped by being a parent to two sons
as he "writhed" to escape his life (p. 140).
Being a parent, Marshfield concludes, is inescape-
able:

> For are not children exactly that
> which does not have an ending, which
> outlasts us, which watches us slide
> over the waterfall, with relief?
> Society in its conventional wisdom
> sets a term to childhood; of parent-
> hood there is no riddance. Though
> the child be a sleek Senator of
> seventy, and the parent a twisted
> husk mounted in a wheelchair, the
> wreck must still grapple with the
> ponderous sceptre of parenthood.
> (p. 141)

Bob Slocum (Heller, 1975) also has trouble
relating to his children: "'I don't have too
much in common with children, not even my own....
I really don't enjoy children'"(p. 133). He feels
isolated from his children--"Something happened to
both my children that I cannot explain and cannot
undo" (p. 164). Slocum's son functions as a mirror
to Slocum himself. The deja vu sensation is very
painful:

> I could never stand to see him taken
> advantage of. It was as though I my-
> self were undergoing the helpless
> humiliation of being tricked, turned
> into a sucker. My own pride and ego
> would drip with wounded recognition...
> He seemed lost and distant and passive
> to me in a way it seemed I had once
> been myself and still feel I am at
> times when my guard lets down and my
> strength ebbs away. (pp. 264-265)

Both Marshfield and Slocum feel responsible for a parent living in a nursing home. Marshfield (Updike, 1975) visits his senile father "once a week in theory, less often in practice" (p. 147). Slocum guiltily decides not to invite his mother to live with them (p. 194). He visits her as a "dutiful son" (p. 296) but with a great deal of resentment. "Why could she not have gone away unnoticed, as my father had done," he asks, "inconveniencing me not at all?" (p. 297).

Slocum yearns for his army days when he had "freedom of choice....I was outside my family, had no wife, job, parent, children, met no one I cared for. I had no ties." (p. 400). He complains that his family presses in upon him too closely (p. 7). He often wishes he "had no dependents. It does not make me feel important to know that people are dependent on me for many things. It's such a steady burden" (p. 422).

Charles Grey (Marquand, 1949) feels pressured to pursue a promotion at the bank in order to provide for his family in style. Feeling he can never really get ahead he envies a friend who has no children. "There was no doubt," he realizes, "that children were hostages to fortune" (p. 492). Telling his son that "this is a pretty tough world" Charles knows that all he could really do was to provide "an illusion of security" (p. 776).

Willy Loman in Death of a Salesman (Miller, 1949) is under pressure to keep up the appearance of being a successful salesman. He worries that he'll never "sell anything again, that I won't make a living for you, or a business for the boys" (p. 38). He struggles with the illusion that he has raised his boys well and cannot understand their lack of material success. The burdens he has assumed hardly seem worth it in the end. "'Figure it out,'" he tells his wife. "'Work a lifetime to pay off a house. You finally own it, and there's nobody to live in it.'" Linda responds, "'Well, dear, life is casting off. It's always that way'" (p. 15).

Godfrey St. Peter (Cather, 1925) is
another protagonist who would like to "cast off"
the responsibilities of middle age. "Life had
been shaped," he muses, "by all the penalties and
responsibilities of being and having been a lover.
Because there was Lillian, there must be marriage
and a salary. Because there was marriage, there
were children" (p. 265). Death is the only
escape for Godfrey--"a release from every obligation, from every form of effort" (p. 272).

The generation squeeze is characterized
by more than a burdensome responsibility. The
protagonists are caught in a bipolar projection
which is psychologically distressing. Projecting themselves into the position of their aging
parents, the men see what they do not want to
become. And projecting themselves towards their
youthful off-spring, they mourn the loss of vitality and youthful promise.

Uncomfortable in his position of mid-life,
Tom Marshfield (Updike, 1975) views both his
father and sons as "menacing foreign objects"
(p. 240). Acutely aware that he may become like
his father, he says, "My father...was in a genetic
dimension unfolding within me, as time advanced,
and occupying my body like...a hand being forced
into a tight glove" (p. 136). His father's aging
bothers him as he sees himself following the same
pattern: "The backs of his hands were spattered
with large moles, ancestors of the moles that had
begun to emerge on the backs of mine" (p. 150).

Marshfield's sons provide an impetus in
Tom's struggle to stay young. His passion for
golf "did not begin shooting in my muscles until
I had an athlete for a son. Nor did I become a
lover until my second son proved beautiful"
(pp. 145-146). His son Martin's virility is
especially disturbing to Marshfield and it is
eventually through sexual encounters that Tom
fights middle age. Picking Martin up from school
one day Marshfield is "startled by a glimpse of
male beauty....I was seeing him with an unusual

50

perspective, as a young male in the world, severed
from me. He was, suddenly quite without intending
it, beautiful" (Updike, 1975, p. 229).

St. Peter (Cather, 1925) claims he does
not understand his daughters and sees their
adulthood as a reflection of his aging: "When a
man had lovely children in his house, fragrant
happy, full of pretty forces and generous impulses,
why couldn't he keep them?" (p. 126).

Babbitt (Lewis, 1922) has little to do
with his mother and in-laws for the encounters are
too painful. "Sometimes he rather liked" his
mother but "he was reduced to pulpiness when she
discoursed about a quiet mythical hero called
'Your Father' (p. 188). He is "bewildered" by his
children's behavior and feels threatened by the
youth and beauty of his son's girlfriend--"dismayed"
and "wretched that she should consider him old"
(p. 184). When Babbitt takes his teenage son on a
business trip he is conscious of the age difference
while at the same time attempting to act like a
young man. He tells the porter on the train:
"'Yes, sir, it's a bad give--away for the old man
when he has to travel with a young whale like Ted
here!'" And he tells his son, "'You stick around
with me, old man, and I'll show you a good time!'"
(p. 197). Babbitt who cannot carry out a rebellion
of his own finally looks to his son for a vicarious
fulfillment of his dreams:

> 'I've never done a single thing I've
> wanted to in my whole life! I
> don't know's I've accomplished any-
> thing except just get along. I
> figure out I've made about a quarter
> of an inch out of a possible hundred
> rods. Well, maybe you'll carry
> things on further. I don't know. But
> I do get a kind of sneaking pleasure
> out of the fact that you knew what
> you wanted to do and did it. Well,
> those folks in there will try to
> bully you, and tame you down. Tell

51

'em to go to the devil! I'll back
you....Don't be scared of the
family. No, nor all of Zenith.
Nor of yourself, the way I've been.
Go ahead, old man. The world is
yours (Lewis, 1922, p. 319).

Dick Diver (Fitzgerald, 1934), conscious
of his parenthood role, wonders what he has to
give to the "ever-climbing, ever-clinging, breast-
searching young? (p. 311). Shannon in The Night
of the Iguana (Williams, 1961) is drawn to the
aged father substitute, Nonno. Shannon is
"fiercely, almost mockingly tender with the old
man--a thing we are when the pathos of the old,
the ancient, the dying is such a wound to our
own (savagely beleaguered) nerves and sensibili-
ties..." (p. 69).

Herzog's (Bellow, 1964) parents are dead
but their influence is very much alive as Moses
tries to sort out his role in relation to them.
Recalling his father near the end of his life,
Moses is stunned by "how much disintegration had
already taken place." He feels confused and com-
pelled to confess to his father--"I aged. I wasted
myself in stupid schemes liberating my spirit"
(p. 304). Moses sentimentally recalls his mother
and desires to tell his wife about her, but
doesn't. She is not interested in Mother Herzog,
he decides, "however mother-bound this nostalgic
gentleman's soul might be" (p. 142). Indeed,
Herzog's failure with his wife is due in large part
to the confusion of roles he plays with her--
father, son or husband, he is never quite sure.

Slocum (Heller, 1975), the business man,
pictures the three generations as "an illustrated
flow chart." At holiday dinners he can see himself "all mapped out inanimately in stages around
the dining room table....I am all their ages.
They are me" (p. 375). Feeling the stress of
bipolar projection Slocum states:

I can transfer myself into my mother's
brother's, sister's past to see my

> present and my future. I shift
> my glance into the future of my
> children and can see my past. I am
> what I have been. I incorporated
> already what I am going to become.
> (Heller, 1975, pp. 375-376)

He sees the irony of fathering a retarded son and
being the son of a dying parent. "My mother
couldn't speak at the end. My youngest child
Derek couldn't speak from the beginning" (p. 332).
And:

> (As my mother faded away, speechless,
> in one direction, Derek emerged,
> speechless, from the other.) And
> there you have my tragic chronicle of
> the continuity of human experience,
> of this great chain of being, and
> the sad legacy of pain and repudi-
> ation that one generation of Slocums
> gets and gives to another, at least
> in my day. (p. 194)

Slocum is distressed by his mother growing older
and more crippled and dying in slow stages and
having shriveled fingers (p. 97). He worries about
his daughter reaching the teen years and he can't
say "I love you" to her because "it sounds like
incest" (p. 179).

Aside from fearing the aging which the
older generation represents through bipolar projection, the protagonists are haunted by their
parents' expectations. Most of the middle-aged
men in this study are well into their careers,
supporting a family and their own parents. Socially and economically independent, they resent feeling directed by what they perceive to be parental
measures of their "success in life." The pressure,
real or imagined, which a mother or father exerts
upon the protagonists is the third property of
the category generation squeeze.

Willy Loman's (Miller, 1949) suffering is

53

made more acute when he is compared to his father. "Father was a very great and a very wild-hearted man" Ben tells him. "With one gadget he made more in a week than a man like you could make in a lifetime" (Miller, 1949, p. 49). Maxine tells Shannon (Williams, 1961) that his troubles are due to rebeling against his mother and God: "You got back at God by preaching atheistical sermons and you got back at Mama by starting to lay young girls" (p. 86).

Tom Marshfield (Updike, 1975) is tortured by failure as a minister, a role he assumed by way of his father's influence. In a poignant visit to his father he confesses, "'Daddy, I am your son, It's me, Tommy. They're sending me away, They say I've disgraced the Ministry'" (p 203). He hopes for forgiveness: "'Something's gone wrong. I have no faith'" (p. 203). "'Tell me what to do,'" he pleads. "'What shall I become? I wanted to become better than you'" (p. 204). Moses Herzog (Bellow, 1964) also feels he has failed his father. On a visit he felt like the "prodigal son, admitting the worst and asking the old man's mercy" (p. 305). And to his mother he writes, "I may turn out to be not such a terrible hopeless fool as everyone, as you, as I myself suspected" (Bellow, 1964, p. 307).

When George Webber in You Can't Go Home Again (Wolfe, 1940) is asked what motivates him to write, he answers:

> 'No one's old man ever went to school
> except under polar conditions. They
> all did. And that's why you get up,
> that's why you drive yourself,
> because you're afraid not to....I'll
> also hear the voice of the old man
> yelling at me from as far back as I
> can remember, and telling me I'm not
> worth the powder to blow me up....
> I'm lazy--but every time I surrender
> to my baser self, the old man hollers
> from the stairs.' (p. 302)

Haunted by what he imagines to be his dying mother's last words "'You're no good'" (p. 510), Bob Slocum (Heller, 1975) battles his way through middle age finally realizing he will never be able to escape her influence:

> I still have these grief-filled dreams about my mother. There's a part of me I can't find that is connected to her still as though by an invisible live wire transmitting throbs. It refuses to die with her, and will continue to live inside me, probably, for as long as I survive. In my final coma, I suppose, even if I live to be a million, my self-control will lapse and I will die moaning, "Ma. Momma. Momma.' (p. 191)

The influence of parents obviously does not cease with their death. Death, however, does bring about a momentary feeling of helplessness. Dick Diver (Fitzgerald, 1934), upon receiving notice of his father's death "sat down on the bed, breathing and staring; thinking first the old selfish child's thought that comes with the death of a parent, how will it affect me now that this earliest and strongest of protectors is gone?" (p. 203). George Webber feels a "sense of loss and unbelief such as one might feel to discover suddenly that some great force in nature had ceased to operate" (p. 41). And Willy Loman (Miller, 1949) asks his brother to stay a few days because "Well, Dad left when I was such a baby and I never had a chance to talk to him and I still feel--kind of temporary about myself" (p. 51).

In summary, the generation squeeze appears to be an important category descriptive of middle-age men. If middle age is viewed spatially, that is, being in the middle of three generations, it can be seen that the protagonists feel burdened by responsibility to parents, children and spouse. It is also a psychologically distressing position, for through bipolar projection they fear becoming

aged while at the same time mourn their lost
youth. The spectre of parental pressure, the
third property of the generation squeeze, contrib-
utes to the distress of men in mid-life.

Career Malaise

The fragmentation which the protagonists
experience as they attempt to cope with middle age
is heightened by feelings of dissatisfaction with
their careers. While young adulthood can be
viewed as a period of career development, middle
age is a time when one senses a plateau has been
reached. Career accomplishments are reviewed,
and goals are reevaluated. In this study, it
appears that even for those who judge themselves
as successful, a mid-life career malaise diminishes
feelings of fulfillment. Some of the men are bored
with their jobs, some are so preoccupied coping
with their age-related problems that they are
temporarily unable to function in their work, and
others feel trapped, too old to make a career
change. The properties of "boredom," "inertia"
and "trapped," captures the essence of the category,
career malaise, as experienced by the twelve protagonists.

Bob Slocum (Heller, 1975), the successful
businessman, finds little satisfaction in his work.
He is intensely bored. "Life," he says, "has
pretty much been one damned sterile office desk
after another" (p. 337). The situation has gotten
worse in middle age:

> I am bored with my work very often
> now. Everything routine that comes
> in I pass to somebody else. This
> makes my boredom worse. It's a real
> problem to decide whether it's more
> boring to do something boring than
> to pass along everything boring that
> comes in to somebody else and then
> have nothing to do at all. (Heller,
> 1975, p. 28)

56

To pass the time Slocum devises "Happiness Charts" in which he ranks employees on the basis of such unhappy traits as envy, fear, ambition, frustration (Heller, 1975, p. 29). He finds the whole operation boring: "Nothing any of us does affects matters much....It's a honeycomb; we drone" (p. 393). In a frustrated outburst he agonizes, "I think, sweet bleeding Jesus," I will "go out of my mind from this fucking job of mine" (p. 169).

Babbitt's (Lewis, 1922) malaise is more subtle. He has trouble identifying the cause of the dissatisfaction and boredom which now pervades his life. After making a large sum of money on a real estate deal, he tells Paul: "Here I've pretty much done all the things I ought to; supported my family and got a good house and a six-cylinder car, and built up a nice little business....And yet, even so, I don't know that I'm entirely satisfied!" (p. 52). Babbitt's restlessness grows:

> As he approached the office he walked faster and faster, muttering, 'Guess better hustle.' All about him the city was hustling, for hustling's sake. Men in motors were hustling to pass one another in the hustling traffic. Men were hustling to catch trolleys....
> Among them Babbitt hustled back to his office, to set down with nothing much to do except see that the staff looked as though they were hustling. (p. 128)

A short sickness gives Babbitt time to reflect: "He beheld, and half admitted that he beheld, his way of life as incredibly mechanical. Mechanical business--a brisk selling of badly built houses" (p. 190). He doesn't want to return to work--"He thought of telephoning about leases, of cajoling men he hated, of making business calls and waiting in dirty anterooms--hat on knee, yawning at fly-specked calendars, being polite to office-boys" (Lewis, 1922, p. 191).

A visit back to his hometown and a talk
with his boyhood friend serves to expose Charles
Grey's (Marquand, 1949) own career. Both he and
his friend had played "according to the rules, and
he had seen the result that night, a pre-ordained
and sterile ending. The worst of it was that it
partially reminded him of his own career" (p. 768).
If Babbitt sees everyone meaninglessly "hustling,"
Grey "could see himself hurrying, always hurrying,
and he would be hurrying again tomorrow back to
Nancy and the children and back to taking care of
other people's money" (p. 770). Mr. Zero in The
Adding Machine (Rice, 1923) has been a bookkeeper
for twenty-five years, "just addin' figgers an'
waitin' for five-thirty" (p. 23). Zero finally
tells his boss, "I ain't quite satisfied. I been
on the job twenty-five years now and if I'm gonna
stay I gotta see a future ahead of me" (p. 38).

Several protagonists also feel a sense of
inertia, a second property of career malaise. The
protagonists find that they cannot motivate themselves to keep working at the pace of their younger
years. Herzog (Bellow, 1964), although "he had
made a brilliant start" and had "several articles
and a book" to his credit, finds that his latest
projects "had dried up, one after another" (p. 11).
He had taken time off to write a book "with a
new angle on the modern condition" (p. 53) but "in
the closet his old valise was swelled like a scaly
crocodile with his uncompleted manuscript. While
he delayed, others came up with the same ideas"
(p. 255). He can no longer work the way he used
to:

> Something had come over him. He used
> to be able to keep going but now he
> worked at about two percent of
> efficiency, handled every piece of
> paper five or ten times, and mis-
> placed everything. It was too much!
> He was going under. (Bellow, 1964,
> p. 151)

Herzog eventually loses sight of just what he was supposed to be writing. "He must live," he says to himself. "Complete his assignment, whatever that was" (Bellow, 1964, p. 283).

Tom Marshfield (Updike, 1975) finds it difficult to function as a minister. He has faith he says, "but it doesn't seem to apply" (p. 203). He realizes that entering the ministry was not in answer to a call but because his father had been one. The parsonage "furniture forced me to do it," he confesses (p. 31). Racked with doubts he asks his mistress, "'How can you believe, Frankie? How can any sane person?'" He goes on:

> 'It's an establishment, Frankie love.
> A racket. Believe me. The words are
> empty. The bread is just bread. The
> biggest sales force in the world sell-
> ing empty calories--Jesus Christ.
> What is it, Frankie? A detergent? A
> deodorant? What does it do, Frankie?
> This invisible odorless thing.'
> (p. 184)

Shannon, in The Night of the Iguana, (Williams, 1961) is another clergyman who can no longer perform in that role. Hannah perceptively characterizes him as "a man of God, on vacation" (p. 71). Shannon admits that he is not able to "conduct services in praise and worship" of a God who is no more than a "senile delinquent" (p. 59).

Willy Loman (Miller, 1949) believes in his worth as a salesman but cannot overcome the inertia brought on by his aging. When his wife assures him that he is earning enough, he responds, "'But I gotta be at it ten, twelve hours a day. Other men--I don't know--they do it easier....I gotta overcome it. I know I gotta overcome it'" (p. 37). Being on the road has become debilitating-- "'I get so lonely--especially when business is bad and there's nobody to talk to. I get the feeling that I'll never sell anything again'" (p. 38).

Inertia characterizes Dick Diver's
(Fitzgerald, 1934) career malaise. "He had only
one or two ideas--that his little collection of
pamphlets now in its fiftieth German edition contained the germ of all he would ever think or
know....Pursued for a year by increasing doubts,"
he decides to write "an introduction to more schol-
arly volumes to follow" rather than begin a new
book (pp. 165-166). Godfrey St. Peter in The
Professor's House (Cather, 1925) also has trouble
writing. He has taken the summer off to work but
finds "he was really doing very little" (p. 262).
And when the fall term of the university opened,
he lacks his usual enthusiasm and interest in
students: "He supposed he did his work....He
found, however, that he wasn't willing to take
the trouble to learn the names of several hundred
new students. It wasn't worthwhile" (p. 271).

Although George Webber (Wolfe, 1940) keeps
writing, it takes him many more years than he had
anticipated to complete his second novel. Pulled
by the weight of inertia, he tells his friend
Randy that he must keep at it because "you're
afraid not to. You work because you have to drive
yourself to such a fury to begin....It's so hard
to get started that once you do you're afraid of
slipping back" (p. 300).

Besides feelings of boredom and inertia,
some protagonists discover that they are also
trapped in mid-life, in mid-career. Marshfield
(Updike, 1975), although realizing that he does
not have the faith to be a minister, feels it is
too late to change careers--"'What else can I do?'"
he asks. "Than be a minister. Than deceive Jane
and keep my appointments. Than be unhappy" (p. 81).
When his mistress Alicia suggests he leave the ministry and come live with her, he asks, "'What would
I do, outside the ministry? It's my life. It's my
afterlife. 'Be a gigolo or a private detective'
Alicia answers. "'Just stop being your own prison-
er'" (Updike, 1975, p. 82).

Slocum (Heller, 1975) wonders why he

continues to work for a man he "hate(s) and
fear(s)" (Heller, 1975, p. 203). The people who
rank highest on his "Happiness Charts"

> are those people, mostly young and
> without dependents, to whom the
> company is not yet an institution
> of any sacred merit....But still
> only a place to work, and who
> regard their present association
> with it as something temporary....
> I put these people at the top
> because if you asked any one of them
> if he would choose to spend the rest
> of his life working for the company,
> he would give you a resounding No!,
> regardless of what inducements were
> offered. I was that high once. If
> you asked me that same question today,
> I would also give you a resounding
> No! and add:
>
> 'I think I'd rather die now.'
> But I am making no plans to leave.
> I have the feeling now that there
> is no place left for me to go. (p. 29)

Near the top of his company, he asks, "is this all
there is for me to do? Is this really the most I
can get from the few years in this one life of
mine?" He answers his own question with an emphatic
"Yes!" (p. 26). Even though bored and feeling
trapped in his job, Slocum is astute at office
politics. It is a game with little meaning--"We
come to work, have lunch, and go home. We goose-
step in and goose-step out, change our partners
and wander about, sashay around for a pat on the
head, and promenade home till we all drop dead"
(p. 26). The American ideal of "upward mobility
is nothing more than a game of Frisbie. We rise
and fall like Frisbies, if we get off the ground
at all" (p. 493).

Charles Grey (Marquand, 1949) complains

about having to go along with the system. His
wife warns him not to "forget" that going after a
promotion is like running for office. "'All right,'
he said. 'I'm not forgetting.' There was no way
to forget, since most of his life ahd been spent
polishing some apple or other. 'If you had to earn
your living, life was a series of apples'"
(Marquand, 1949, p. 411). He finds being promoted
to vice-president of the bank as hollow a victory
as was Slocum's promotion:

> There was a weight on Charles again,
> the same old weight....In spite of
> all those years, in spite of all his
> striving, it was remarkable how little
> pleasure he took in final fulfill-
> ment....The whole thing was contrived,
> as he had said to Nancy, an inevit-
> able result, a strangely hollow climax...
> it was not what he had dreamed.
> (p. 791)

   Babbitt (Lewis, 1922) wishes he could "quit
the whole game" (p. 22). Babbitt's rebellion in-
cludes taking stock of his job prospects: "He
wondered what he could do with his future. He was
still young; was he though with all adventuring?
He felt that he had been trapped..." (p. 316).
Feeling a "slave to his employees, "he had to
expose his back to their laughter, and in his
effort to be casually merry he stammered and was
raucously friendly and oozed wretchedly out of the
door" (p. 61).

   Zero in The Adding Machine (Rice, 1923) is
also enslaved by his work. Wanting to escape he
asks "What chance have I got--at my age? Who'll
give me a job?" (p. 61). He is reprimanded for
such thoughts--"Pull yourself together and calm
down. You can't change the rules--nobody can--
they've got it all fixed. It's a rotten system--
but what are you going to do about it?" (p. 61).

   In at least three cases the sense of being
trapped comes partly from the protagonists' mid-
life realization that they have been pursuing a

career not of their own choice. The money Babbitt
has made in real estate fails to compensate for
the loss of prestige he feels he would have had
as a lawyer and politican (Rice, 1923, pp. 75;
125). Slocum (Heller, 1975) wants "another chance"
because, he says, "I never became what I wanted
to be, even though I got all the things I ever
wanted including two cars and two color TV sets"
(p. 319). Finally, Marshfield (Updike, 1975) feels
he "had no choice but to follow my father into the
ministry" (p. 31), a career which has resulted in
one long "feast of inconvenience and unreason"
(p. 28).

Thus, for the protagonists of this study,
the career malaise is part of the fragmentation
of middle age. While all experience various degrees
of boredom, some (Babbitt, Webber, Slocum, Marshfield, Zero) can at least function in a minimally
satisfactory way. In the more acute cases (St. Peter,
Diver, Herzog, Loman, Shannon), the men are
immobilized, unable to overcome inertia brought
on by their predicament. And most feel trapped,
believing it is too late to change their occupations. Career malaise is another issue these
men in mid-life must confront.

Ego Rejuvenation

The fragmentation of mid-life can be a
lonely and painful process. The loss of bearings
which occurs in the search for meaning, the dynamics of the generation squeeze, the inertia related
to a career diagnosis and the awareness of aging
itself result in the protagonists' need to revital-
ize their lives. For these men, the desire to
remain youthful manifests itself in at least two
ways--through the mentor relationship and through
sexual activity. Middle-aged men are in a unique
position to be mentors. By mid-life most have
achieved, through experience, the status and power
younger men aspire to. Rarely, if ever, is a
young person a mentor, and herein lies the
dilemma for middle-aged men: one cannot be both

young and yet have accumulated the years of experience necessary to offer guidance to others.
Assuming the role of mentor to a younger man
allows for the middle-aged man to operate from a
coveted position of authority, while at the same
time vicariously reliving young adulthood. Sexual
activity, the second dimension of ego rejuvenation,
is yet another hedge on aging. Equating sex with
the virility of young adulthood, most of the
protagonists engage in extra-marital affairs, and
temporarily, at least, feel revitalized. The
following section explores the mentor relationship
and sexual activity as properties of the category,
ego rejuvenation.

Charles Grey's (Marquand, 1949) dealings
with Tom Joyce illustrate the rejuvenating qualities implicit in the mentor relationship. Joyce
is a new employee at the Stuyvesant bank, "fresh
out of the Harvard Business School...one of the
bright young men, as Charles had been when he was
twenty-six" (p. 432). Though he finds Joyce "too
eager and impatient, as he had been once himself,
too anxiously, openly competitive," Grey found it
"very pleasant to have anyone look at him as Tom
Joyce did" (p. 432). Grey sees in Tom "a reflection of his own early enthusiasm, his own desire
to sacrifice to get ahead, staring back at him
over a gap of fifteen years" (p. 432). Grey is
reminded of the time when he himself had been a
mentee--"Charles was about to ask what else he
wanted but stopped when he saw the other's face and
the guileless admiration in it. It was exactly the
way he had looked at Arthur Slade in the old days"
(p. 433).

For Godfrey St. Peter (Cather, 1925) being
a mentor is also rejuvenating. "Just when the
morning brightness of world was wearing off for
him, along came Outland and brought him a kind of
second youth" (p. 258). Through the guidance of
Outland's studies, the professor "had been able
to experience afresh things that had grown dull
with use. The boy's mind," he notes, "had the
superabundance of heat which is always present

where there is rich germination. To share his thought was to see old perspectives transformed by new effects of light" (Cather, 1925, p. 258).

Babbitt (Lewis, 1922) enjoys playing the mentor role to several young men. In dealing with a younger employee, Babbitt finds it necessary to lecture on the work ethic--"being a man given to oratory and high principles, he enjoyed the sound of his own vocabulary and the warmth of his own virtue. Today he had so passionately indulged in self-approval that he wondered whether he had been entirely just" (p. 61). Speaking of the employee, Babbitt says: "oughtn't to call him so hard. But rats, got to haul folks over the coals now and then for their own good" (p. 61). Babbitt finally must fire the young man. He replaces him with another mentee--"Young Fritz was a curly-headed, merry, tennis-playing youngster. He made customers feel welcome to the office. Babbitt thought of him as a son, and in him had much comfort" (p. 195).

Babbitt is sought after by Overlook, a young social climber. Overlook "had admired Babbitt's good-fellowship in college, had admired ever since his power in real estate, his beautiful house and wonderful clothes. It pleased Babbitt" (p. 164). Although not much older than his best friend Paul, Babbitt assumes the role of mentor to him also:

> but always he thought of Paul
> Riesling, with his dark slimness, his
> precisely parted hair, his nose-
> glasses, his hesitant speech, his mood-
> iness, his love of music, as a younger
> brother, to be petted and protected.
> (p. 36) ....He was an older brother to
> Paul Riesling, swift to defend him,
> admiring him with a proud and credu-
> lous love passing the love of women.
> (p. 50)

Whether being a mentor feels like being an older brother or a father to a son as Tony is to

Joe in <u>They Knew What They Wanted</u> (Howard, 1924, p. 131), advice--giving is an important function of the position. Tom Marshfield (Updike, 1975) has taken the training of his assistant minister to heart. "I offered him a lesson in practical religion" (p. 78) he says at one point. "My love for this man took a submissive form" Tom explains. I "wanted him to be wise. I wanted him to grow" (p. 109). Marshfield monitors Ned's development, not always agreeing with Ned's liberalism: "Ned's queerness, I also thought, was, in the developing pan of his new confidence, becoming less shadowy, emergying as a faintly fussy and rococo edge for his gestures and dress" (p. 171).

Middle age is a time when a man ceases being a mentee and becomes a mentor to someone younger. George Webber in <u>You Can't Go Home Again</u> (Wolfe, 1940) offers insight into this role shift. As a young writer George relies heavily upon his editor/mentor Foxhall Edwards:

> The older man was not merely friend but father to the younger. Webber, the hot-blooded Southerner, with his large capacity for sentiment and affection, had lost his own father many years before and now had found a substitute in Edwards. And Edwards, the reserved New Englander, with his deep sense of family and inheritance, had always wanted a son but had had five daughters, and as time went on he made George a kind of foster son. Thus, each, without knowing that he did it, performed an act of spiritual adoption. (p. 340)

As Webber enters middle age he writes a letter to Edwards in which he breaks the mentor relationship. "I was lost" he writes Edwards,

> Perhaps that is one reason, Fox, why for so long I needed you so desper- ately. For I was lost, and was

> looking for someone older and wiser
> to show me the way, and I found
> you....In our nine years together
> you did help me find the way, though
> you could hardly have been aware
> just how you did it, and the road
> now leads off in a direction con-
> trary to your interest. (Wolfe, 1940,
> p. 554)

George Webber finds he has begun to assume the role
of mentor to younger writers: "'Honest, Mr. Webber'",
one mentee wistfully muses, "if I could get somebody like you to help me with this story--to write
it down for me the way it ought to be--'" (p. 324).

Thus being a mentor with its rejuvenating
and tutelage dimensions is one way men in middle-
age deal with the aging process. This relationship
allows them to exercise the prerogatives of middle
age while vicariously enjoying the benefits. Main-
taining virility through sexual exploits represents
another mechanism by which middle-aged males attempt
to assure themselves of their youthfulness.

Dick Diver (Fitzgerald, 1934) has an affair
with Rosemary, a woman considerably younger than
himself. He is conscious of their age difference--"'
Look,'" he tells her, "'I'm in an extraordinary
condition about you. When a child can disturb a
middle-aged gent--things get difficult'" (p. 94).
Rosemary causes Dick to try water skiing feats he
had grown too old to do. Dick's wife senses what
is happening:

> She knew, though, that he was
> somewhat tired, that it was only the
> closeness of Rosemary's exciting
> youth that prompted the impending
> effort--She had seen him draw the same
> inspiration from the new bodies of
> her children and she wondered coldly if
> he would make a spectacle of himself....
> This physical showing-off for Rosemary
> irritated her. (pp. 282-283)

For Dick, Rosemary is a "little wild thing" whose
body was "calculated to a millimeter to suggest a
bud yet guarantee a flower" (Fitzgerald, 1934,
p. 104)

George Babbitt's (Lewis, 1922) sexual ad-
ventures begin with visions of a "fairy child."
"Where others saw but George Babbitt, she dis-
cerned gallant youth....She was so slim, so white,
so eager!   She cried that he was gay and valiant"
(p. 6).   Babbitt searches for the cause of his
restlessness and finally "stumbled into the admis-
sion that he wanted the fairy girl--in the flesh"
(p. 221).   His next step is to find a willing young
woman.   Rebuffed in making a pass at his stenogra-
pher, he seeks out Louetta Swanson, "pretty and
pliant" (p. 104) and the wife of one of his friends.
Failure there leads him to try again with the mani-
cure girl in his barber shop.   In this unsuccessful
venture, he realized "he was turning toward youth,
as youth" (Lewis, 1922, p. 229).   It isn't until
he rents an apartment to Tanis, middle-aged and
available, that he is able to experience his fairy
girl--"in the flesh."   Tanis introduces him to the
Bohemian life style, "studio parties" and "wild
lovely girls" he had been seeking (p. 223).   For
awhile Babbitt enjoys his rebellion--"To be the
'livest' of them was as much his ambition now as
it had been to excel at making money, at playing
golf, at motor-driving, at oratory, at climbing
to the McKelvey set" (p. 274).   Tanis becomes just
a symbol of his attempted rejuvenation--"He perceived that, since he was making love to every
woman possible, Tanis was no longer his one pure
star, and he wondered whether she had ever been
anything more to him than A Woman" (p. 275).   The
"wild evenings" he admitted, were "his last despairing fling before the paralyzed contentment of
middle-age" (p. 308).

Mr. Zero (Rice, 1923) longs for an affair
but is afraid that going with women will get him
into trouble (p. 44).   Speaking of women he says,
"I've seen lots I'd like to grab like that, but
I ain't got the nerve" (p. 44).   Shannon's (Williams,
1961) problems with his congregation begin with

his seducing a young parishoner and continue in
his job as a tour guide:

> Maxine: Why do you want the young
> ones--or think that you do?
> Shannon: I don't want any, any-
> regardless of age.
> Maxine: Then why do you take them,
> Shannon? (He swallows but does not
> answer.)--Huh, Shannon.
> Shannon: People need human contact,
> Maxine honey. (Williams, 1961, p. 22)

Ego rejuvenation through sexual exploits
causes problems for Willy Loman (Miller, 1949) and
Tom Marshfield (Updike, 1975). It is Biff's discovery that Willy has a lover in Boston which creates
an irreparable chasm in the father-son relationship.
Tom Marshfield (Updike, 1975) is sent to a desert
retreat for erring ministers confessing that he
"did sleep with a few, by way of being helpful"
(p. 162).

Tom Marshfield finds his first affair rejuvenating. "Alicia in bed was a revelation. At
last I confronted as in an ecstatic mirror my own
sexual demon" (p. 43). "What fun my forgotten old
body turned out to be" (p. 43). Once Tom realizes
he has the sexual stamina of a younger man, he
reacts with a calculated obsessiveness, seducing
the many females who come to him for counseling.

Slocum (Heller, 1975) is sexually active
with his wife, numerous girlfriends and prostitutes.
Yet he is still concerned about his ability to perform. Recalling his youth, Slocum says "I often
wish I were driven now by that same...mixture of
blind ardor, haste, and tension." Sex is "tame
now, rather predictable and matter-of-fact" (p. 111).
Admitting that "I don't enjoy adultery, really, I'm
not even sure I enjoy getting laid" (p. 260) Slocum
continues his frantic pursuit of women, perhaps
fearing he will lose his power (p. 318). Plagued
by all kinds of sexual fears, he has nightmares of
castration (p. 148) and wonders if he is "the only

middle-aged man in the world who still contains within himself his distant childhood fear of homosexual rape" (Heller, 1975, p. 378).

Herzog (Bellow, 1964) is most conscious of his age when he is with Ramona, his young, vivacious lover. Thinking of her caused him "a little envy of the young" (p. 380) and "he feared being caught in the part of the aging, conceited handsome man" (p. 21). It is through Ramona that Herzog comes to terms with his own sexuality. He worries that his sexual powers have been damaged by his second wife and that "without the ability to attract women, how was he going to recover?" (p. 12). A male friend tells him not to expect much anymore because "guys at our time of life must face facts....After forty it's all the same. If you can get it up once a week, you should be grateful" (p. 106). Fearing that he cannot sexually satisfy Ramona, he rationalizes that he had never really been "the young and glossy stud....There were more faithful worshippers of Eros than Moses Elkanah Herzog" (Bellow, 1964, p. 191). Finding that he is able to respond to Ramona, he is delighted with himself. Embracing her on the street, he says "Since when did middle-aged men behave so passionately in public places?" (p. 253). Ramona reassures him that he is still young--" an old man smells old. Any woman can tell you....But Moses, you are chemically youthful" (p. 243).

Thus, for the males in this study, sexual potency is a prime factor in attempting to regain the vitality of their younger years. The rejuvenation derived from sexual exploits is, at best, temporary. Some escapades lead to trouble (Babbitt, Marshfield, Loman, Shannon); some protagonists (Diver, Herzog, Slocum, Babbitt) find that sexual perigrinations only verify the aging they wish to avoid. Nevertheless, the middle-aged males of this study engage in sexual activity as one means of attempting to cope with their aging.

Summary

Middle age is a period of adult development difficult to pinpoint chronologically or biologically. Middle age is best defined in terms of the psycho-social dynamics unique to the middle part of the life span. An inductive comparative analysis of male protagonists in twelve works of fiction uncovered five categories and their properties characteristic of middle age. The categories and properties are:

(1) The awareness of aging characterized by a reordered time perspective, a concern with physical deterioration confirmed by peers and/or spouse, and intimations of mortality;

(2) A search for meaning in which the protagonists question their lives and feel a loss of bearings;

(3) The generation squeeze wherein the men feel pressured from both ends of the life span (the younger and older generation). The men feel burdened by their responsibility to parents, spouse and children and are made more acutely aware of their aging through bipolar projection--that is, desiring the vitality of youth while at the same time dreading the deterioration of old age. The men also feel pressured by parental expectations;

(4) A career malaise in which their chosen occupation no longer holds the interest or challenge that it did in young adulthood. Careers are found to be boring, energies are dissipated by inertia, and several feel trapped, too old for career change;

(5) Ego rejuvenation, which represents an attempt to recapture one's fading youth and manifests itself through the mentor relationship and/or extra-marital sexual activity.

Coping with these demands of mid-life presents a challenge to the protagonists. It is a time of fragmentation, a time when the various

71

segments of one's life are sectioned out and evaluated. While some form of fragmentation or conflict is a theme characteristic of grappling with
all stages of life, middle age fragmentation can
be differentiated from other life stages by its
own distinctive psycho-social events. The
middle-age categories and properties identified
in this study, though presented individually, are
in reality interactive and interrelated. The
particular configuration and interrelatedness of
these factors create varying amounts of stress
upon the protagonists. Some find coping with their
aging to be relatively easy; for others, the
fragmentation they experience is devastating. Consequently, some are able to restructure their lives,
allowing for continued growth and development,
while others fail to come to terms with the tasks of
mid-life. The next chapter will analyze how the categories of middle age are related, as well as explore the protagonists' approaches to restructuring
their fragmented lives.

CHAPTER IV

INTEGRATION AND RESTRUCTURING
DURING MIDDLE AGE

The fragmentation of mid-life is a process by which certain segments of a man's life come under close and critical scrutiny. This study of twelve middle-aged male protagonists revealed five segments or categories of mid-life. For the purpsoe of analysis and illumination, each category and its defining properties was examined separately. In reality, however, the protagonists did not grapple with each variable separately. The abstracted categories and properties of middle age do not stand in isolation from one another, but are in fact, interrelated and overlapping.

In A Month of Sundays (Updike, 1975), the several concerns of mid-life combine to exert pressure on the protagonist. Tom Marshfield has reached his forties and worries about his physical appearance. At the same time when he is concerned with his own aging, he becomes aware of both the physical beauty of his son and the deteriorating condition of his father. He cannot go back to youth, neither does he want to go forward in age. Stalled in mid-life, Marshfield focuses in on himself and his career as a minister. No matter which segment of his life he surveys, the prognosis is unsatisfactory. He suffers, he says, from the "human condition" (p. 8). The simultaneous awareness of aging, the generation squeeze, and undertaking a search for meaning and a career malaise leave him feeling trapped:

> Again the staircase rose before me,
> shadow-striped to suggest the great
> back of a slave; this time the pre-
> sentment so forcibly suggested to me
> my own captivity, within a God I
> mocked, within a life I abhorred,

within a cavernous unnameable sense of
misplacement and wrongdoing, that I
dragged a body heavy as if wrapped in
chains step by step upward. (p. 103)

Most of the protagonists would probably
agree with Slocum's (Heller, 1975) statement that
"so much of misfortune seems a matter of timing"
(p. 297). The misfortune or unhappiness that they
feel is a result of several interlocking fragments
of middle age simultaneously preoccupying their
thoughts. Slocum's attention, for example, jumps
from concern with his physical deterioration to
family and work responsibilities, back to the
awareness of his aging:

I've got bad feet. I've got a jaw-
bone that's deteriorating and some-
day soon I'm going to have to have
all my teeth pulled....I've got an
unhappy wife to support and two
unhappy children to take care of....
I've got eight unhappy people working
for me who have problems and
unhappy dependents of their own.
I've got anxiety; I suppress
hysteria....I've got old age to
face. My boy, though only nine,
is already worried because he does
not know what he wants to be when
he grows up. My daughter tells
lies. I've got the decline of
American civilization and the
guilt and ineptitude of the whole
government of the United States to
carry around on these poor shoulders
of mine. (p. 61)

Thus, rather than scrutinizing segments of
their lives sequentially, the protagonists grapple
simultaneously with the several aspects of life
which have previously provided purpose and
direction to their existence. The task can be
burdensome.

Although at any one time it might appear
that a single aspect of life preoccupies the protagonist, the various components of middle age are
continuously interactive. Most of Mr. Zero's (Rice,
1923) problems with his family and himself stem
from an overriding and intense boredom brought on
by twenty-five years as a bookkeeper. Likewise,
Tom Marshfield's (Updike, 1975) acute sense of the
generation squeeze combined with the awareness of
aging propels him into an attempt at rejuvenation
through sexual promiscuity.

Herzog (Bellow, 1964), highly intelligent
and introspective, is preoccupied with the search
for meaning. "Herzog had been overcome by the
need to explain, to have it out, to justify, to
put in perspective, to clarify, to make amends"
(p. 8). He realizes and dreads the "depths of
feeling he would eventually have to face" (p. 19).
He tells the reader: "Thus I want you to see how
I, Moses E. Herzog, am changing" (p. 205). As
part of his intense search, Moses takes stock of
his body, his success and failures as a son,
husband and father, and his career as a professor
and author. The deeper he goes in his self
analysis, the more he loses touch with reality,
and the less productive he is in his career.
Herzog's experience, as well as that of several
other protagonists, suggests the hypothesis that
the more one loses bearings, the greater the
sense of career inertia. St. Peter in The
Professor's House (Cather, 1925), for example,
fails to do any work on a new book as he loses
himself one summer in a melanchology search for
meaning. Shannon in The Night of the Iguana
(Williams, 1961), slides into a complete mental
breakdown and cannot function as either clergyman
or tour guide.

A review of the data also indicates that
if a close peer or spouse is experiencing an
awareness of aging and fragmentation of mid-life,
then the protagonist's awareness of aging is more
acute. Babbitt's (Lewis, 1922) crisis is fore-
shadowed and hastened by his friend Paul's middle-

aged problems. And Babbitt's wife and mistress exhibit the physical aging that he is afraid to face. Slocum (Heller, 1975) also finds his wife is going through the same fragmentation that he is experiencing. This causes him to feel even more burdened and also heightens his own awareness of his situation. Shannon (Williams, 1961) finds little solace for his problems in the middle-aged Maxine, or with the old poet Nonno who recites verses about youth.

A third tentative hypothesis can be extracted from a review of the interrelatedness of the categories and properties of middle age. It appears that if one's career is very unsatisfactory, then the responsibility associated with being the middle generation is more burdensome. Escape from a boring job is precluded by the protagonists' sense of obligation to the many family members dependent upon them for financial support. Babbitt (Lewis, 1922), for example, admits that his dream of being a lawyer or politician was thwarted by an early marriage. His responsibilities as husband and then father prompted him to build a thriving real estate business. With success came a high standard of living. In mid-life Babbitt finds himself bored by his job and terribly oppressed by having to maintain an affluent life style, not so much for himself, but for his wife, demanding teenage children, and aging parents. Grey (Marquand, 1949), Slocum (Heller, 1975), and Loman (Miller, 1949) also find little joy in their work and so feel oppressed by having to continue to provide.

The generation squeeze which affects these protagonists is a concept unique to middle age. The uniqueness of the middle position can be better understood by exploring its relationship to two additional categories. For example, a middle-aged person's search for meaning appears to be different from that of either the young or the elderly. A young person's search for identity is in terms of who he or she is to become. An older person reviews a total life with little thought to undertaking major changes in his or her few remaining years. While the younger generation is future oriented and the older generation is retrospective, being the middle generation necessitates accounting for the past and the future as well as the present. The search for meaning requires an analysis of all that has accumulated before mid-life as well as projecting one's future direction. The middle-aged protagonist finds he has left neither the unlimited years of youth, nor the few years of the elderly. He has instead, a measured amount of time which somehow must be lived in a meaningful way.

Being the middle generation also has special significance in terms of the protagonist's awareness of aging. The physical development of youth is towards becoming a mature adult. The aged's physical concerns are with deterioration. The middle-aged protagonist must come to terms both with the decline of youthful vigor and with signs of the anticipated physical deterioration of the future.

Thus the process of fragmentation with its interrelated variables creates tension for the protagonists. Some are able to function with moderate effectiveness, while others find coping more difficult. In order to free themselves from the debilitating effects of mid-life fragmentation, a restructuring, or rehabilitation of their lives must take place. Some of the men are able to come to terms with their aging and redirect their lives in a productive manner. Others fail. Only through restructuring, however, is future growth and development possible.

Restructuring

The data suggest that of those men able to cope with the tasks of this life stage, restructuring occurs in two ways: (1) after experiencing a period of fragmentation some protagonists decide that, for them, adopting a new life style or mode of thought is too disruptive; rather, they resign themselves to their aging, their family and their career and go on in much the same way as before; or (2) the men endure this period of conflict and fragmentation and as they work through it forge a new outlook or perspective on life which will guide them in the future.

Babbitt (Lewis, 1922) is one protagonist who finally resigns himself to his situation and carries on in much the same pattern as before his rebellion. His desperate desire to break from his mid-life position and accompanying responsibilities has resulted in his having an affair, drinking and carousing with "the bunch." After an argument with his wife in which he refuses to make excuses for an evening excursion, he thinks to himself--"I'm going to keep free. Of her and Tanis and the fellows at the club and everybody. I'm going to run my own life!" (p. 295). He finds, however, that "running" his own life means relinquishing the old ways, something he cannot quite do:

> He was afraid to go to lunch at the Athletic Club, and afraid not to go. He believed that he was spied on; that when he left the table they whispered about him. Everywhere he heard the rustling whispers: in the offices of clients, in the bank when he made a deposit, in his own office, in his own home. Interminably he wondered what they were saying of him.
> He could not stand the strain. Before long he admitted that he would like to flee back to the security of conformity, provided there was a decent and creditable way to return. (p. 301)

He vacillates between enjoying his new lifestyle
and missing the security of the old: "Babbitt was
uncomfortable. He felt a compulsion back to all
the standards he had so vaguely yet so desperately
been fleeing" (p. 277).

The road back to his former life as a
"Good Citizen" comes by way of his wife's sudden
sickness:

> Instantly all the indignations which
> had been dominating him and the
> spiritual dramas through which he
> had struggled became pallid and
> absurd before the ancient and
> overwhelming realities, the standard
> and traditional realities, of sick-
> ness and menacing death, the long
> night, and the thousand steadfast
> implications of married life. (Lewis,
> 1922, p. 305)

He realizes, with some regret, that there will be
no more "wild evenings," that "this had been his
last despairing fling before the paralyzed contentment of middle age" (p. 308). Sympathy from
his social group for his wife's illness allows
him the period of grace necessary to return to the
fold--"Then did Babbitt, almost tearful with joy...
at being permitted to stop fighting...cease
utterly to be a domestic revolutionist" (p. 310).
He realizes that he has been "licked," "trapped
into the very net from which he had with such fury
escaped and, supremest jest of all, been made to
rejoice in the trapping" (p. 316). Babbitt turns
to his son as a means of fulfilling his own desires
for a free life--"I do get a kind of sneaking
pleasure out of the fact that you knew what you
wanted to do and did it....The world is yours!"
he tells Ted (p. 319).

Mr. Zero (Rice, 1923) and Charles Grey
(Marquand, 1949) are two other protagonists who
put the pieces of their lives back in much the
same manner as before. Zero is a white-collar

nonentity, bored with job, wife and friends, but
lacks the courage to break out of the middleclass,
middle-age constraints, even in an afterlife.   In
a satirical caricature of heaven, Zero discovers
that he is the archetypal slave--"The mark of the
slave was on you from the start," he is told by
Charles, one of heaven's "lieutenants" (Rice, 1923,
p. 60). He is doomed to being tied to a "superb,
super-hyper-adding machine" (p. 61) in his next
reincarnation. He accepts the inevitable, especially when he learns he will have a girl named
Hope to keep him company.

        In a conversation with his wife, Grey
(Marquand, 1949) tries to articulate his frustrations: "'I wish we weren't always being pushed
around. I'd like for once in my life to be able
to tell someone to go to hell'" (p. 500). He too,
lacks the motivation to effect a change and specu-
lates, "the harder you pursued happiness, the less
liberty you had, and perhaps if you pursued it
hard enough, it might ruin you" (p. 770). Not as
brave as Babbitt, Grey takes no chances to
jeopardize his opportunities for a bank promotion.
There is little satisfaction in becoming vice-
president--the struggle had been "superficial"
(p. 779), he complains, the victory "inevitable"
and "strangely hollow" (p. 791). Grey moves on in
life, resigned to his situation.

        Several other protagonists restructure
their lives more creatively. Through the fragmentation and restructuring of mid-life, they evolve
a new perspective which provides hope and meaning
for the future.

        Moses Herzog (Bellow, 1964) methodically
tries out several strategies in an attempt to come
to grips with his mid-life crisis. Turning first
to his intellect, Herzog tries to reason his way
out--"believing that reason can make steady progress from disorder to harmony and that the con-
quest of choas need not begin anew each day"
(p. 225). His intellectual pursuit of a "grand
systhesis" (p. 255) doesn't work"

But then he realized that he did not
need to perform elaborate abstract
intellectual work--work he had
always thrown himself into as if
it were a struggle for survival.
But not thinking is not necessarily
fatal. Did I really believe that
I would die when thinking stopped?
(Bellow, 1964, p. 324).

This attempt to cope through using other
people does not work either. He makes frantic
visits to old friends, to relatives, to new
friends. This method offers him little solace.
"In the midst of it [explaining his problem] the
realization would come over him that he had no
right to tell, to inflict it, that his craving for
confirmation, for help, for justification, was
useless" (p. 194). He finally realizes that "the
best thing he could do was to stop asking people
for advice and help" (p. 267).

Literate and intellectual, Herzog falls
back upon his own inner strengths to resolve his
dilemma. He secludes himself in the country and
writes letters which are never sent. "Nature...
and I are alone together, in the Berkshires, and
this is my chance to understand" (p. 388). Of his
letter writing he says "more words. I go after
reality with language" (p. 332). He analyzes the
human condition. He rejects loneliness as being
"simply the plankton on which Leviathan feeds"
(p. 379). He also rejects suffering as a means of
illuminating the human condition--"More commonly
suffering breaks people, crushes them, and is
simply unilluminating" (p. 386). He argues against
Nietzsche's stand that mankind must "live with the
void" (p. 389).

His self-therapy begins to work. "Brother-
hood" he decides, "is what makes a man human"
(p. 333). He gradually frees himself--"Joy! His
servitude was ended, and his heart released from
its grisly heaviness and encrustation" (p. 381).
He writes to his friend that "the remission of

81

pain is no small part of human happiness" (p. 381).
His resolution is one of humanistic synthesizing--
"'I mean to share with other human beings as far
as possible and not destroy my remaining years in
the same way.' Herzog felt a deep, dizzy eager-
ness to begin" (p. 392).

Godfrey St. Peter (Cather, 1925) is another
professor who feels the need to be alone as he
tries to understand the malaise which has overtaken
him. He reviews his life, trying "to account for
the fact that he now wanted to run away from
everything he had intensely cared for" (p. 275).
While his family tours Europe, Godfrey spends the
summer reminiscing about his youth. His melancholy,
he realizes, is caused by the recognition that he
is no longer young, that in fact, he is growing
old:

> Coming upon a curly root that thrust
> itself across his path, he said
> 'That is it.' When the maple leaves
> along the street began to turn
> yellow and waxy, and were soft to
> the touch,--like the skin on old
> faces,--he said: 'That is true; it
> is time.' All these recognitions
> gave him a kind of sad pleasure.
> (p. 266)

He feels he is nearing the end of his life (p. 267)
and welcomes a release from responsibilities. A
close encounter with death, however, snaps him
out of his depression. He finally understands the
reason for his troubled spirit and symbolically
buries his youth--"His temporary release from
consciousness seemed to have been beneficial. He
had let something go--and it was gone: something
very precious, that he could not consciously have
relinguished" (p. 282). He has restructured with
understanding. He knew that "he was not the same
man" his family "had said good-bye to....He felt
the ground under his feet. He thought he knew
where he was, and that he could face with fortitude
the future" (p. 282).

Sensitive and artistic, George Webber
(Wolfe, 1940) moves from young adulthood to middle-
age with a full awareness of himself and his development. He has spent four years writing his second
book, exploring he writes, "the jungle depths of
Brooklyn-jungle depths coincident with my own
soul" (p. 572). Of that time he says, "I was
also more involved than I had ever been before
with my inner struggle. Those were the years of
the greatest doubt and desperation I had ever
known" (p. 561). He had wanted, he confesses "what
all men want in youth: to be famous, to be loved"
(p. 559). He achieves both fame and love and finds
neither fulfilling. Moving from the self-absorption
of youth he confesses a desire to "see things
whole" (p. 318). His restructuring is a process
of growth--"My life, more than that of anyone I
know, has taken on the form of growth" (p. 572).
Webber comes to a humanistic orientation similar
to that of Herzog--"I was coming more and more to
feel an intense and passionate concern for the
interest and designs of my fellow men and of all
humanity" (p. 561).

Bob Slocum's (Heller, 1975) restructuring
is violent and cathartic. His-mid life problems
are compounded by an inability to let go of his
youth. "When I grow up," he reveals, "I want to
be a little boy" (p. 319). Slocum's son becomes
the focus of his distress. He sees the boy as
himself: "And hiding inside me somewhere, I
know....is a timid little boy just like my son who
wants to be his best friend and wishes he could
come outside and play" (p. 213). Slocum transfers
some of his own unhappiness to his son--"so I made
him unhappier still (purging myself of some of
my own distress in the act of doing so)" (p. 265).

Resolving his crisis through action, Slocum
"accidentally" smothers his son as he comforts him
following a car accident. In this brutal and
violent act, he symbolically purges or kills the
boy-self within him. He has fulfilled a recurrent
dream that his boy will die: "He perishes, but the
tragedy in my dreams" says Slocum (Heller, 1975),

"is always mine" (p. 146). With the death of the
child, Slocum is able to cope with the responsibilities of manhood. "Systematically," he says,
"I am putting my affairs in order" (p. 527). At
work "people seem dazzled by the swift competence
with which I appear to be taking things under control" (p. 527). His wife is happier, his daughter
has stopped telling lies (p. 527).

Thus, the restructuring which is necessary
for the protagonists' continued growth occurs
through either a decision to accept one's situation
and make the best of it, or through achieving a new
perspective on the world, which will guide the
second half of their lives. There are some men who
can do neither. The failure to reconstruct out of
fragmentation halts any further development.

Failure to Restructure

Diver (Fitzgerald, 1934), although realizing that "the totality of life may be different in
quality from its segments" (p. 245), cannot seem
to put the pieces back together. "His work became
confused with his wife's problems" (p. 170), he
feels a "new coldness in his heart" (p. 168),
and realizes "I'm not much like myself anymore"
(p. 256). Living the life of the rich, Dick
begins drinking as a way of coping with his problems. Alcohol hastens his deterioration. He tells
Nicole-"'I can't do anything for you any more. I'm
trying to save myself'" (p. 301). He tells Rosemary
that he has "gone into a process of deterioration"
(p. 285). Remorseful and alcoholic, Dick cares
little that he loses his wife to another man. He
finally leaves the Riviera and goes back to America.
Nicole reports that he "opened an office in
Buffalo, but evidently without success" (Fitzgerald,
1934, p. 314). Dick's life has become one of
drifting and depression (p. 315).

Shannon, the defrocked minister in The
Night of the Iguana, (Williams, 1961) is self-
absorbed and intensely lonely as he journeys into

84

the self. Religious faith no longer anchors him
to reality. He warns a girl on the tour that she
should not get mixed up "with a man in my unstable
condition....I don't have a dime left in my
nervous emotional bank account--I can't write a
check on it, now" (p. 53). Looking at the iguana
tied under the veranda, he says to Hannah, "See
The iguana? At the end of its rope? Trying to
go on past the end of the goddam rope? Like you!
Like me! Like Grampa with his last poem!" (p. 120).
Shannon tries "to go on, to continue, as if he'd
never been better or stronger in his whole existence" (p. 26). He cannot or will not halt his own
disintegration, however, and must finally hand
himself over to the care of Maxine.

An inability to cope leads one protagonist,
Willy Loman (Miller, 1949), to suicide. Feeling
too old and tired to be on the road, he fails in
his efforts to be reassigned to an office job.
His sons have not turned out the way he had hoped,
and he feels burdened by having to maintain the
image of a successful salesman. After several
attempts to pull himself together, he ends his
life, an escape which he has apparently contemplated
for some time.

Tom Marshfield (Updike, 1975) is sent to a
desert retreat for a month of therapy and recuper-
ation. The therapy, which consists of rest and
daily journal writing, appears to work. He writes
four sermons, one for each Sunday, in which he
progresses from defiantly justifying the adultery
he has so wantonly engaged in (p. 52), to asserting
man's need for redemption (p. 246) in the last ser-
mon. His self-absorption is ending and he can at
last relate to the other men at the retreat:

> Imperceptibly these errant and bank-
> rupt clergymen have replaced the
> phantoms that chased me here,
> phantoms it now seems my heart had
> conjured from its own fevers, had
> bred like fungi in an unlit dank

> of self-absorption. This desert
> sun has baked them away. (Updike,
> 1975, p. 235)

However much it appears that Tom is moving towards a resolution, there are clues throughout his therapeutic journal that his "solution" will be to postpone an inevitable confrontation between his role as a minister and his promiscuous life style. On his last night he says "I went out under the dome of desert stars and was afraid, afraid to be born again" (p. 269). On the morning of departure he says "My life...seems all loose ends...I cannot cope" (p. 270). "I am preparing for some leap," he says. The backwards version of the leap that brought me here?" (p. 223). The book ends with Tom sexually seducing the woman in charge of the retreat (pp. 270-271). He has failed to deal with his age-related problems. In his role as a minister a collision course looms ahead.

The data from this study suggest that restructuring is necessary for continued growth and development. Those protagonists who cannot redirect themselves become alcoholic, suffer a breakdown, or commit suicide. Other protagonists are eventually able to cope, some more creatively than others, with the fragmentation of middle age. Babbitt, Zero, any Grey find their middle-age and middle-class life style too comfortable to leave. They restructure by resigning themselves to the lives they had forged as young men. Herzog, Slocum, St. Peter and Webber, all articulate, sensitive and intellectual protagonists, are able to endure the analysis of the segments of middle age, can confront their aging, and thus restructure in meaningful ways.

In summary, what has emerged from this analysis of twelve fictional men is a paradigm of middle age which in turn explains their mid-life behavior. Fragmentation and restructuring necessitate a grappling with an awareness of aging, a search for meaning, the generation squeeze, a career malaise, and ego rejuvenation. Fragmentation occurs as the protagonists begin to experience the properties inherent in one or more of the categories. The mutual interdependency and interrelatedness of the categories compound the men's feelings of discomfort and distress. In a desire to restore some harmony and tranquility in their lives, they attempt to piece the segments together, sometimes by transforming them. Those who are successful at restructuring are able to face the second half of their lives with some measure of peace.

CHAPTER V

COMPARISON OF FINDINGS WITH PSYCHO-SOCIAL RESEARCH AND DISCUSSION OF LITERATURE AS A DATA SOURCE

In this study of twelve middle-aged male protagonists, grounded theory data analysis techniques were applied to literary materials for the purpose of generating new insights into male middle age. The first section of this chapter compares the findings of the study with the findings of psycho-social research. The comparison reveals to what extent this study's findings confirm what is already known through empirical research, as well as the extent to which this study uncovered new insights. Secondly, the utility of literature as a data source for generating knowledge of adult development will be assessed. The chapter concludes with an evaluation of the efficacy of grounded theory research techniques as applied to literary materials.

Comparison to Psycho-Social Research

A comparison of this study's findings to psycho-social research can best be achieved by first dealing with the categories and the properties of middle age. The explanatory framework of fragmentation-restructuring will then be compared to the broader psycho-social theories of middle age.

Several of the categories and properties of mid-life uncovered in this study confirm empirical findings. A reordered time perspective, concern with physical deterioration, intimations of mortality, the search for meaning, and career malaise have been found by other researchers to be characteristic of middle age.

Neugarten (1968b), in lengthy interviews of 100 middle-aged men and women found that "both sexes, although men more than women, talked of the new differences in the way time is perceived. Life is restructured in terms of time-left-to-live rather than time-since-birth" (Neugarten, 1968b, p. 97). Gould (1972), in his study of adulthood, found that discrimination between age groupings could be made in terms of the subject's sense of time, as well as attitudes toward self and others. In the age group 35-43 there is an increasing awareness of a "time squeeze." "The sense of time during this stage," he writes, "emphasizes the finitude of time and there is an eye toward the past, present, and future equally" (p. 526). Referring to the same age group, Kuhlen (1968) notes that coming to the realization that time and life are not infinite "probably has quite a significant effect upon one's orientation and motivation" (p. 118). Nearly all of the protagonists in the present study experienced a reordered time perspective which in turn had an impact on the other aspects of their lives.

Concern with physical deterioration was found to be a substantive characteristic of all twelve protagonists. The psycho-social literature is fairly conclusive on this point also. Levinson's study of men (1974) revealed that a sense of bodily decline and aging are major issues of mid-life. That this finding is perhaps more applicable to males is supported by Neugarten's discovery (1968b) that many men in her sample described "bodily changes as the most salient characteristic of middle age" (p. 96). Interesting, too, is her finding that middle-aged women engage in "body-monitoring" of their husbands. While not extracted in this study as a category pertinent to middle-aged men, several of the wives do assume this function. Mrs. Babbitt prods her husband to eat lighter lunches and to stop smoking (Lewis, 1922), the professor's wife tells Godfrey that he ought to take more care of his health (Cather, 1925), Linda worries that Willy Loman will wear himself out as a traveling salesman (Miller,1949), and so on.

Intimations of mortality, another property of the awareness of aging, finds some support from clinical practice and empirically based studies. Jacques (1965), a psychoanalyst, found the mid-life problems of his clients precipitated by a fear of death. In mid-life, he says, "we encounter the onset of the tragedy of personal death with the sense of grief appropriate to it." Death, he notes, "instead of being a general conception...becomes a personal matter, one's own death, one's own real and actual mortality" (p. 512). Lowenthal (1975), in a large field study of four age cohorts of adulthood, did not find a fear of death, but did find that thoughts of death become more personal as one ages (p. 229).

This study found that all but one of the protagonists, Tony, in They Knew What They Wanted (Howard, 1924), engaged in a search for meaning. The questioning of one's life appears to be an integral component of middle age. Gould (1972) found his mid-life subjects engaged in "an existential questioning self, values, and life itself" (p. 526). As compared to students, newlyweds and preretirees, Lowenthal's (1976) middle-age sample were more involved in a life review. Neugarten (1968b) noted that introspection and self-analysis emerged as a prevailing theme of middle age. Some form of "critical self-assessment" (Buhler, 1968, p. 164) has also been reported by Levinson (1968), Sears (1973), Jacques (1968), and Jung (1971).

As part of the awareness of aging and its accompanying search for meaning, the protagonists experience a dissatisfaction with their careers. Most of the protagonists feel bored, a sense of inertia and/or trapped. In the empirical literature, men, more than women, define themselves in terms of their career, and middle age is a time for review. By mid-life most men have reached a plateau and stock is taken of their accomplishments to date (Lowenthal, 1975; Buhler, 1968). Slotkin's study (1952) of careers in middle age found that an unsatisfactory evaluation can lead to suicide, hedonism or redirection. In this study, Willy Loman's suicide and Marshfield,

Slocum and Babbitt's hedonistic pursuits can be tied, at least in part, to their career frustrations. That the inertia and trapped sensations of career are related to middle age is supported by Kuhlen's (1968) studies on motivation:

> A middle-aged or older person may feel threatened and insecure because of skill deficits generated by rapid technological advance that has left him outdated....
>
> Fifth, and finally, is the greater threat and frustration that people may encounter because of their inability to do anything about some of the disturbing circumstances and sources of unhappiness which they experience. A person tends to get 'locked in' particular circumstances as he marries, has children, invests in property, accumulates training and seniority, and may find himself unable to move out of a frustrating situation from which the younger uncommitted individual could easily free himself. (p. 118)

In summary, the fictional literature used as a data source in this study did in fact generate several findings congruent with psycho-social investigation. Of the five major categories, elements of three--awareness of aging, the search for meaning and a career malaise--duplicated findings by the researchers on middle age. That literature can also be used to uncover new insights into a period of adult development is seen by an analysis of the other findings of this study.

The generation squeeze, as defined by the properties of oppressive responsibility, bipolar projection and parent pressure, is a major finding of this investigation. The uniqueness and also the distress associated with being the middle of three generations is only alluded to in the psychosocial literature. Neugarten (1968b) noted that the "middle-ager sees himself as the bridge between generations" (p. 94). She explores this factor in terms of the distance--"emotionally, socially and culturally"--the middle-ager feels between himself, the young, and the old'(p. 94). Lowenthal (1975) found conflict between parents and teenage children most trying for the middle-aged and preretirement samples (p. 41). Havighurst (1952) listed assisting teenage children to become responsible adults, and adjusting to aging parents as two developmental tasks of middle age. However, no systematic or analytical exploration of the repercussions of being the middle generation could be found in the psycho-social research. It appears that the sensitizing aspects of feeling oppressed by responsibility to all the generations, as well as the psychological stress associated with bipolar projection, are new findings.

Another contribution this study makes to knowledge of adult development is an exploration of the mentor relationship. Vaillant (1977b) found that young men have mentors, but deals with the phenomenon from the point of view of the mentee, rather than the mentor (p. 41). Levinson (1976), in his study of the developmental patterns of men aged 18 to 45, explains the mentorship role of middle-aged men in terms of Erikson's concept of generativity. The mentor, Levinson says, "cares, sponsors, criticizes, and bestows his blessing. The teaching and sponsoring have their value, but the blessing is the crucial element" (pp. 23-24). While this study of literary protagonists also found the advice-giving, tutelage dimension of the role, the data strongly suggested that middle-aged men become mentors because of its rejuvenating value.

Peer/spouse confirmation of the aging process is yet another new insight uncovered in this investigation. All but one of the protagonists experience a heightened awareness of their own aging through observing or listening to a close friend or spouse. A survey of the psycho-social literature for evidence of this phenomenon turned

93

up only one reference. Speaking of the period
35-43, Gould (1972) notes that "under the time
pressure of conflict and questioning, the person
looks to the spouse, who is often in a similar
life position and is looking for the same support" (p. 526). Other than noting its occurrence, Gould does not investigate its meaning.

Thus, the comparison of this study's categories and properties to psycho-social findings
on middle age attests to the fact that literature
can generate new insights as well as confirm and
elaborate existing knowledge. The literature
provided sensitizing and explanatory insights
into what it means to be the middle of three generations, what one function of the mentor relationship might be, and the importance of peer/spouse
confirmation of one's aging.

While empirical research has uncovered
defining characteristics of the mid-life period of
development, there are very few theorists who have
integrated the specifics into a inclusive explanation. Those who have postulated a theoretical
framework have done so within the context of
either the entire life span or all of adulthood.
A comparison of this study's broad conceptual
framework that middle age is a period of fragmentation and restructuring will, of necessity, focus
upon the middle age segments of life-span or adult-
span theories.

Jung (1971) theorizes that the stages of
life unfold in relation to the structure and dynamics of the psyche. Middle age is a period "full
of problems" which present "the possibility of a
widening of consciousness" (p. 4). It is the
task of the adult to leave the security of youth
and face the problems of a growing consciousness:

> Every one of us gladly turns away
> from his problems; if possible, they
> must not be mentioned, or, better
> still, their existence is denied....
> We want to have certainties and no

doubts--results and no experiments--
without even seeing that certain-
ties can arise only through doubt
and results only through experi-
ment....When we must deal with
problems, we instinctively resist
trying the way that leads through
obscurity and darkness. We wish
to hear only of unequivocal results,
and completely forget that these results can only be brought about
when we have ventured into and
emerged again from the darkness.
(Jung, 1971, p. 5)

Jung (1971) goes on to explain that "the meaning
and purpose of a problem seem to lie not in its
resolution but in our working at it incessantly.
This alone preserves us from stultification and
petrifaction" (pp. 11-12). The fragmentation-
restructuring paradigm presented in this study can
be compared to Jung's thesis that growth in mid-
life necessitates grappling with its problems.
This can only be done if one relinquishes the
protective shield of youth, something that the
protagonists in this study have trouble doing.

As noted earlier, it is the interrelatedness and interplay of the dynamics of mid-life
which affect the protagonists' behavior. Jung
(1971) also noted that "behavior is due...to the
circumstance that man's psyche is a unique combination of factors which are at the same time the
special subjects of far-reaching lines of research"
(p. 6).

Of the eight stages of man in Erikson's
theory, the stage of generativity versus stagnation
coincides with middle age. According to Erikson
(1952), successful negotiation of this life stage
means achieving a "favorable ratio" of generativity
over stagnation (p. 274). This results in the
virtue of caring. At this stage of life a person
must become other-centered. To not "accept the
responsibility which evolution and history have

given him," results in the individual's "mental
deformation of self-absorption" (Erikson, 1964,
pp. 130-131). Erikson is not specific as to the
process involved in achieving a generative orientation. A comparison can be drawn, however,
between the protagonists of this study who fail
to restructure and the inability to become generative. The restructuring process explored in this
study involves confronting and accepting the obli-
gations and responsibilities of middle age as well
as developing a "widening concern for what has
been generated by love, necessity, or accident"
(Erikson's definition of Care) (Erikson, 1964,
p. 131). Webber's growing awareness of a world
outside of himself, St. Peter's and Herzog's development of a humanistic orientation are good
examples of this. Likewise, Diver and Shannon,
who cannot restructure, illustrate the self-
absorption characteristic of stagnation.

Peck (1968) is one psychologist who has
concentrated on developing a theoretical framework
to explain middle age and old age. Expanding
Erikson's generativity versus stagnation concept,
Peck postulates four dichotomies for middle age:
valuing wisdom versus valuing physical powers,
socializing versus sexualizing in human relationships, cathetic flexibility versus cathetic impov-
erishment and mental flexibility versus mental
rigidity. As with Erikson's generativity, the
restructuring element of this study's paradigm can
be compared to achieving a positive balance of
the crucial elements in Peck's theory. All of the
protagonists, for example, desire to cling to the
physical powers of youth and are concerned with
physical deterioration. Peck (1968) found in a
personality analysis of persons who were mostly
businessmen, that "to rely on physical powers
which they no longer possess(ed)" resulted in the
subjects becoming "increasingly ineffective in
their work roles and social roles" (p. 89).
Herzog, St. Peter and Marshfield exhibit such
ineffectiveness. Likewise, Babbitt, Slocum,
Shannon and Marshfield all have problems in their
human relationships as they emphasize sexualizing

rather than socializing.

Buhler (1968) divides the human life span into five phases roughly parallel to biological development. She has incorporated these phases into a theory which emphasizes an individual's goal-setting strategies. Young adulthood, middle age and old age are equivalent to expansion, culmination and contraction in activities and accomplishments. Goals which are set in youth are fulfilled and/or re-examined in middle age. Subsequent research by her student, Frenkel-Brunswik (1968), revealed that the transition which occurs during middle age is "marked by psychological crisis" (p. 80). Buhler's and Frenkel-Brunswik's work encompass the life span and so do not explore in depth the dynamics of this transition phase. Certainly, though, the fragmentation-restructuring process experienced by the twelve fictional men of this study was painful and distressing, analogous, perhaps to the crisis of the transition phase.

Kuhlen (1968) integrates the middle age segments of career analysis, decline in physical energy, changing time perspective and self-appraisal into a life-span model of expansion-contraction. Growth-expansion motives of the first half of life give way to anxiety and threat as motives for the second half of life. The emergence of the contractive motives of anxiety and threat occurs sometime in mid-life. The process of fragmentation and the need for restructuring in order to continue to develop could explain the period of shift from Kuhlen's early life motives to those of later life.

Gould (1972), Levinson (1974) and Vaillant (1977) are other researchers who have investigated adult development over the life span. Working mostly with male samples and heavily influenced by Freudian psychology, their theorizing presents a few points for comparison with the theoretical framework of this study. Gould (1974) found that

97

the conflict and questioning of 35-43 year olds gave way to a resignation and "mellowing" in the 40's and 50's (Gould, 1974, p. 526). Levinson (1974) noted that the crisis of the mid-life transition is followed by "restablization" in which "a new life structure begins to shape and provide a basis for living" (p. 255). Vaillant (1977) saw the lives of his male samples in terms of their ability to cope in middle age as well as other stages of life. The success one had with coping depended upon the adaptive mechanisms employed by each man. The ways in which the protagonists of this study restructured or failed to restructure could be viewed in terms of the adaptive mechanisms each one used.

This section has attempted to compare the theoretical framework of fragementation and restructuring, which encompassed the mid-life behavior of the protagonists of this study, with theories derived from empirical research or clinical observations. With the exception of Peck's, the major theoretical models of Jung, Erikson, Buhler, and Kuhlen deal with the entire life span. For the purpose of comparison, the period relevant to middle age was extracted and reviewed in terms of the fragmentation-restructuring model presented in this study. Because of the life span perspective of these theorists, a separate explanatory paradigm is not presented for the middle age segment. And what is presented is best understood by viewing it within the total framework of their theories. Neugarten, and to some extent Levinson, have concentrated on middle age per se. Their research, however, has generated descriptive characteristics of middle age rather than an integrated theory. Neugarten's findings of the salient issues of middle life were relevant for the comparison with the categories and properties of this study.

In summary, the comparison of both categories and properties as well as the paradigm of middle age generated by a literary data source has proved revealing. Several categories were found to duplicate empirical findings, and

parallels could be drawn between the fragmentation-restructuring model and elements of the
major theories of the life cycle. That this study
also generated some new insights which could be
integrated into an explanatory paradigm supports
both the use of literature as a data source, as
well as the techniques of grounded theory research.

Literature as a Data Source

One of the objectives of this study was
to explore the utility and validity of literature
as a data source for generating knowledge about a
period of adult development. The comparison of
this study's findings to those of psycho-social
research revealed that literature can offer support for empirically-based knowledge as well as
uncover new insights about male middle age. It
could be argued, in fact, that two new findings--
the meaning of the generation squeeze and peer/
spouse confirmation of aging--were discovered
perhaps because of the use of literature as a data
source. That is, the protagonists of this study
were seen by the researcher within the full context of their lives. Being able to observe their
interaction with family members, friends and co-
workers provided a rich scenario of interpersonal
relationships from which peer/spouse confirmation
and elements of the generation squeeze could be
extracted. This is also true to some extent for
the explanation of the mentor relationship. All
three of these characteristics of middle age
require interaction between the protagonists and
other people.

Another advantage in using literature as
a data source is that the concerns of the protagonists are articulated well, either by the men themselves, by the authors in a third person narrative,
or through a combination of approaches. Thus, for
the analyst, the data are richly "sensitizing."
For example, Slocum's musing in Something Happened
(Heller, 1975) that he had "changed the position
of a fetus for the position of a corpse" (p. 318),

99

Marshfield's noting in A Month of Sundays (Updike, 1975) that "heredity works up as well as down" (p. 145), and Sinclair Lewis (1922) telling us that Babbitt hustled to his office and sat down "with nothing much to do except see that the staff looked as though they were hustling" (p. 128), vividly illustrate middle-aged characteristics of a reordered time perspective, bipolar projection and career boredom. Thus literature, as an artistic and creative expression of an aspect of the human condition, provides the researcher with vivid data for first generating, and then illustrating the elements of an inductive theory.

Some further observations can be made with regard to the specific literary works of this study. Six works from post World War I and six works from post World War II were selected for investigation. The works represent a fifty-year time span in twentieth century American society as well as differences in literary style. Table I on page 101 reveals that there was no significant difference between the two time periods with regard to the richness of the works for generating insights into male middle age. The literary works of the post World War I era exhibited a total of 56 instances illustrative of the middle-age categories and properties for an average of 9.3 per literary work. The post World War II era works presented 64 instances for an average of 10.7 per literary work. From this observation it would appear that characteristics salient to middle-age men have remained constant in twentieth century America. Also, it appears that extracting information about a period of human development does not depend upon literary style. This can be demonstrated further by comparing the property of sexual activity which was found to be a means of ego rejuvenation. The protagonist's sexual exploits are much more explicitly described in the post World War II literature. However, four of the six post World War I protagonists also exhibited this characteristic. The rejuvenating quality of the property, in fact, was first discovered in the researcher's reading of Tender is the Night

TABLE 1

DISTRIBUTION OF THE CATEGORIES AND PROPERTIES IN THE LITERARY WORKS

	AWARENESS OF AGING				SEARCH FOR MEANING		GENERATION SQUEEZE			CAREER MALAISE			EGO REJUVE-NATION		TOTALS
	Reord. Time Persp.	Conc. Phys.	Intim. of	Peer/ Spouse	Quest. of	Los. Bear.	Oppr. Resp.	Bipol. Proj.	Par. Press.	Bore-dom	Iner-tia	Feels Trap.	Mentor Rela.	Sex Activ.	
1. THE PROFESSOR'S HOUSE (Godfrey St. Peter)	X	X	X	X	X	X	X	X			X		X		10
2. TENDER IS THE NIGHT (Dick Diver)	X	X		X	X	X	X	X	X		X		X	X	11
3. BABBITT (George Babbitt)	X	X	X	X	X	X	X	X		X	X	X	X	X	13
4. YOU CAN'T GO HOME AGAIN (George Webber)	X	X	X	X	X	X	X		X	X	X		X		11
5. THEY KNEW WHAT THEY WANTED (Tony)		X											X	X	3
6. THE ADDING MACHINE (Mr. Zero)	X	X		X	X	X					X	X		X	8
7. Herzog (Moses Herzog)	X	X	X	X	X	X	X	X	X		X			X	11
8. SOMETHING HAPPENED (Bob Slocum)	X	X	X	X	X	X	X	X	X	X		X		X	12
9. POINT OF NO RETURN (Charles Grey)	X	X	X	X	X	X	X					X	X		9
10. A MONTH OF SUNDAYS (Tom Marshfield)	X	X	X	X	X	X	X	X	X	X	X	X	X	X	14
11. DEATH OF A SALESMAN (Willy Loman)		X		X	X	X	X	X	X		X			X	9
12. THE NIGHT OF THE IGUANA (Shannon)	X	X		X	X	X		X	X	X				X	9
TOTALS	10	12	7	11	11	11	9	8	7	5	8	5	7	9	

(Fitzgerald, 1934), a post World War I novel.

Differences in literary style and historical period appeared to have little effect on a work's usefulness as a data source. In this study, however, literary genre did make a difference, with novels proving to be significantly more productive than drama. The eight novels contained a total of 91 occurrences of the properties of middle-age for an average of 11.4 per work. The four plays contributed only 27 occurrences for an average of 6.8 per work. In other words, for the purpose of this study, novels proved to be nearly twice as helpful as plays. The two post World War II plays--Death of a Salesman (Miller, 1949) and The Night of the Iguana--(Williams, 1961) were better sources of information than the two post World War I plays, but were still less helpful than any of the novels. They Knew What They Wanted by Sidney Howard (1924) provided no insights and only minimal support for this study's findings. The play is a sentimental exploration of the marriage between Tony, an aging wine grower, and Amy, a waitress and mail-order bride. The marriage event provides a vehicle for the author's characterization of Tony and Amy. The plot's narrow focus and the emphasis upon characterization restricted the attention given to issues related to middle age. On the other hand, no evidence was found in this play which either contradicted or modified findings generated by the other literature.

One other minor observation can be made with regard to the works used in the study. The length of the novels and the plays appeared to have little bearing on their usefulness. Babbitt (Lewis, 1922), which is at least twice as long as A Month of Sundays (Updike, 1975) was not twice as helpful. Both were equally good data sources for geneating insights and verifying emerging categories.

While observations regarding differences in historical period, style, genre and length

of the works are suggestive, much more literary
research needs to be done before firm generalizations can be made about the importance of such
factors in using literature as a data source.
This study does attest to the fact, however, that
literature offers promise for generating knowledge
about a period of human development.

With regard to using literature to explore
male mid-life, another issue needs to be addressed
and that is the extent to which the demands of
literature necessitate placing a protagonist in a
conflict or crisis situation. For most fiction,
action is generated by the ways in which a protagonist reacts to and attempts to resolve a conflict. Undoubtedly, there are happy, middle-aged
men who experience little if any stress in mid-
life, but there would be little interest in reading
about them. The fictional works in this study
explore the problematic dimension of mid-life and
generalizations to all middle-aged men must be
made with considerable caution. Within this limitation, a great amount of variation was found
among the protagonists with regard to the severity
of their situation. The fragmentation the men
experienced as they grappled with the demands of
mid-life ranged from being mildly disturbing to
traumatic. If "crisis" is defined with the popular
connotations of a time of intense turmoil and
distress, then several of the protagonists could
be categorized as being in a "mid-life crisis"
(Marshfield, Slocum, Herzog, Shannon). Other
protagonists, while experiencing stress as a result
of middle-age related problems, would not fall into
a "mid-life crisis" category (St. Peter, Webber,
Zero, Grey). And just as the literature presented
a continuum of stress, there was also great variation in the ways in which the men coped with their
problems.

The fact that these literary works explore
the more problematic dimension of middle age does
not, however, preclude their usefulness as a data
source for uncovering insights into male mid-life.
Rather, the authors' exaggeration of the human

103

condition actually facilitates the extraction of the salient issues of mid-life. It is these psychosocial factors such as an awareness of aging, search for meaning, generation squeeze, and so on, which are the important findings of the study and more applicable (than the crisis aspect) to middle-aged men in general. Shakespeare's King Lear is a good case in point. As an overdrawn portrait of an old man, it is hardly descriptive of the great majority of older persons. This factor, however, does not detract from the play's universal and timeless appeal as an expression of certain salient issues of old age. Thus, even when an aspect of the human condition is exaggerated, fiction can still provide universal insights. As Berger (1977) has recently claimed:

> Such insights are convincing and worthy of further investigation for several reasons. First, they ring true; that is, they conform to the reader's general sense of things, to their common sense about themselves as social being. Frequently insights also follow from the events and characters the novelist describes, from the premises in the story, all of which are felt to resemble real experience in some way. Readers thus accept the novelist's conclusion from his premises as applying to social life outside as well as inside the story. (p. 161)

In exploring the question of the usefulness of literature as a data source, it was pointed out that this investigation both supported empirical knowledge and generated new insights. While novels were found to be generally more useful than plays, there was little difference between the post World War I and post World War II works. Literature thus appears to be a potentially valuable source of information about adult development. Grounded theory research can provide the techniques necessary to carry out a systematic inquiry.

Analysis of Grounded Theory Research Techniques

This study of male middle age was unique in two ways: (1) literary works were used as the data source and (2) the research methodology of grounded theory provided the analytical framework for the inquiry. Literature could have been utilized to uncover insights into a period of adult development without being coupled with a systematic research methodology. However, a more impressionistic and less disciplined investigation might offer little guidance to future investigators and the results, in all possibility, would be highly idiosyncratic. Likewise, use of a deductive research model might have produced verification of a pre-conceived paradigm, but it probably would not have uncovered any new insights into male middle age. As pointed out by Lindauer (1974), using literature to study psychology requires the use of innovative methodology:

> A suitable balance between the rigor of scientific method and the scope of literary material has to be achieved. The solution may be reached through ingenious research designs and techniques. The intransigence of literary materials to objective study offers an opportunity to find new models of research....There can be a pluralism of methodology; whatever contributes to a knowledge of human nature, including the personal, natural, historical, subjective, and observational documents of literature, should be part of scientific psychology. (p. 54)

Grounded theory research offered the potential for discovery of new knowledge as well as provided systematic data analysis techniques which could be employed by other researchers.

As discussed in the "methodology" chapter, the basic strategy in grounded theory research is the constant comparative method of data analysis. This technique worked well in its application to the literary works in this study. Categories, properties and tentative hypotheses emerged simultaneously with the collection, coding and analysis of data. In addition, a skeletal theory inspired by Dick Diver's (Fitzgerald, 1934) observation on the "segments of life" (p. 245) emerged about one third of the way through the research. This tentative framework as well as emerging categories provided focus for further data collection. McBee key sort cards, which provided instant access to the data, were found to be extremely helpful in coding and analyzing data as well as in writing the results.

In grounded theory research the emphasis is on discovery, with verification and description as secondary concerns. Since the major objective of the study was to discover insights into male middle age, grounded theory methodology appeared to be well-suited to the goals of this research. This emphasis on discovery, however, poses a potential drawback. While the researcher, using a deductive, hypothesis-testing model can describe his/her step-by-step verification procedures, discovery is not a process which lends itself to mechanical explanation. Insights derived from the data, the "discovery" of a category or property depend, to a large extent, upon the sensitivity and analytical powers of an investigator who must also have "an appetite for exploration and a tolerance for ambiguity" (Darkenwald, 1978, p. 10). This is perhaps particularly true when applied to a literary data source. While trying to uncover salient issues of middle age from fiction, a researcher must be able to sift through extraneous descriptive material, as well as interpret metaphorical allusions which may be presenting a relevant point.

It is also conceivable that another researcher could systematically analyze the same literary works and "discover" other categories, properties, and hypotheses. This, however, would not detract from the validity of this study's findings unless the results were contradictory. Rather, the theory produced by each study would be judged by its overall explanatory power, its logical consistency, and the extent to which findings were faithfully generated from the data. Indeed, a data source as rich as literature would seem to present many opportunities for discovery. And while the act of discovery itself cannot be explained, grounded theory research does provide through the constant comparative technique of data analysis, one tool which makes discovery possible.

In conclusion, the data analysis techniques of grounded theory research applied to the literary works of this study seem to the researcher to be useful for meeting the major objective of the research--that of generating new knowledge and insight into the male mid-life period of development. The coupling of literature with an inductive research methodology also provided a prototype for further research into human development.

CHAPTER VI

SUGGESTIONS FOR FURTHER RESEARCH
AND IMPLICATIONS FOR PROGRAM DEVELOPMENT
IN ADULT EDUCATION

Suggestions for Further Research

This study of men in mid-life coping with their aging uncovered new insights as well as some which are well supported by empirically based studies. Future researchers might find it fruitful to operationalize the new findings and test them empirically. As Berger (1977) points out:

> Many fictional insights may be stated in the form of propositions or hypotheses about human behavior and social institutions, or of historically limited conclusions about events or social classes, or of moral judgements about the lessons or meaning of human experience....Finally, there do exist historical and social-science studies, tested by the evidence according to the best methods that scholars have been able to devise, with which to test in turn the insights found in novels. (p. 161)

In particular, the generation squeeze and the mentor relationship are two findings from this study which invite further research. The social, psychological and economic ramifications of being the middle generation are related to other aspects of a person's life. For example, one might investigate the extent to which the feelings of oppressive responsibility are related to career dissatisfaction. It would seem that those who are bored in their work would feel more burdened by social and economic responsibilities to parents and children than those who enjoy working and providing.

109

It might also be postulated that the assistance of extended family members living close by might lessen the "squeeze" or pressure of being mid-generation as opposed to being mid-generation in a nuclear family network. It would be interesting, too, to compare the extent to which middle-aged women, especially if they are not the primary source of income, feel the generation squeeze.

The stress associated with bipolar projection in which the middle-ager envies the physical vitality of youth and fears the deterioration seen in the older generation, would seem to be related to an awareness of aging. Thus, a researcher could investigate the relationship between one's concern with physical deterioration (a property of the category awareness of aging) and bipolar projection.

Several empirical studies have identified the mentor relationship and its advice-giving dimension. This study uncovered a new aspect of the relationship--that the process of mentoring is also rejuvenating. This discovery (that is, the rejuvenating qualities of mentoring) could be explored further. For example, one could investigate whether the shift from being a mentee to becoming a mentor occurs in conjunction with a recorded time perspective. The question might also be raised regarding the extent to which career satisfaction depends upon whether or not one is a mentor.

Most research (this study included) has approached the mentor relationship from either the young man's (mentee's) point of view or the middle-aged (mentor's) perspective. The total process of mentoring including the interrelationship between the younger and older person needs to be investigated further. Finally, the questions of whether the mentor relationship develops within blue-collar occupations and the existence and nature of mentoring between women might be studied.

Using a sample of middle-aged men, the interrelationships between other categories and properties generated in this study could be operationalized and tested. The data seemed to suggest, for example, that aspects of career malaise and the search for meaning are related. Likewise, it is probable that a man who seeks rejuvenation through activity is more concerned with his physical aging than a man who accepts his aging. Another approach for further research might be to investigate the sex differences or socio-economic differences in the occurrence and nature of a category such as awareness of aging.

Thus, the findings of this study, especially those which have not been identified or adequately documented before in the psycho-social research literature, present many opportunities for further study. Literature appears to be a rich source for generating insights which can then be operationalized and tested.

Much further research can also be done using literature as a data source. With regard to the substantive area investigated in this study--middle-aged male development--other literary genres such as poetry, autobiography or short stories could be explored for their usefulness in generating insights. "The Love Song of J. Alfred Prufrock" a poem by T. S. Eliot (1958), for example, portrays a middle-aged man searching for meaning, bored with life, and concerned with his aging. Pertinent sections of biographies and autobiographies, a non-fictional genre, could be analyzed for information about middle age as well as provide longitudinal data on the entire life span. A major theorist of the life cycle, Charlotte Buhler (1968), successfully used autobiographies and biographies for determining stages of human development.

Aside from further study on middle age via different literary genres, other segments of the life span could also be investigated through literature. Adolescence, young adulthood, and

111

old age have all been captured in well known
fictional works such as J. D. Salinger's <u>The
Catcher in the Rye</u> (1951), James Joyce's <u>A
Portrait of the Artist as a Young Man</u> (1964), and
Ernest Hemingway's <u>The Old Man and the Sea</u> (1952).

A study similar to this one might focus
on female protagonists. It would be interesting
to discover what insights might emerge from an
analysis of the women in Edward Albee's <u>Who's
Afraid of Virginia Woolf?</u> (1963), Tennessee
Williams' <u>A Streetcar Named Desire</u> (1947), or
Theodore Dreiser's <u>Sister Carrie</u> (1961). Even
further, a comparison could be made between the
stages of development for men and women. How are
they the same, and how are they different?

Another problem for comparative analysis
would be to investigate a segment of the life span
through literary works from different historical
periods. What differences might there be between
an 18th century middle-aged protagonist's concerns,
and the concerns of a protagonist from the 20th
century?

A study of middle-aged men from the literature of American subcultures might also be illuminating. It would be interesting to investigate
how membership in a minority group might affect the
concerns of a particular period of adult development. Cross-cultural comparisons could be equally
as fruitful. Would a Chinese middle-aged protagonist, for example, feel threatened by aging as
the protagonists here were, or look forward to
becoming old in view of that culture's reverence
for the elderly? Likewise, would an African
protagonist experience a generation squeeze,
given African familial and tribal associative
patterns? These types of investigations might
illuminate the ways in which the social-psycholog-
ical dynamics of any age segment are culturally
determined.

One might also take several works by one
author and either investigate all the mid-life

characters for example or trace the different stages of development portrayed in the works. To illustrate, Shakespeare's plays could be examined with the aim of extracting characteristics of middle age. They could also be read for the purpose of analyzing differences between Hamlet's young adulthood, Antony's middle age, and King Lear's old age.

Using grounded theory research methodology, other aesthetic data sources such as film and paintings could be explored for insights into periods of human development. Speaking of the relationship between science and art, Lindauer (1974) notes that "a basic source of communality between many of the sciences and the arts is that both begin with a concern and questioning about man and end with answers and achievements related to this common focus" (p. 44). The protagonist of Bergman's "Scenes From a Marriage" could be studied for insights about middle-aged men. Erik Erikson (1976), to illustrate rather than build theory, compared the life cycle of the film protagonist in "Wild Strawberries" with Erikson's stages of life.

In summary, if one can agree with Glaser and Strauss (1967) that theorizing is based on one's own insights or the "borrowed experience of others," (p. 252) then literature presents an almost unlimited data source for investigation. Further study of adult development can be undertaken with different literary genres, different social and historical milieus, and with a focus on the different stages of human development. Used in combination with the data analysis techniques of grounded theory research, this type of investigation holds much promise for making significant contributions to the understanding of adult development.

Implications For Adult Education

Just as knowledge of child development has guided educational programming for youth, so too, understanding adult development can be an asset in planning adult educational programs. This study investigated one dimension of adulthood--that of the male middle age crisis. Based upon the findings of the research, several suggestions can be made for developing meaningful educational experiences for this segment of the population.

This study found that men experience a career malaise in mid-life. It is a time when some, if not most men pause to evaluate what has been accomplished to date. The assessment process is important in terms of how men continue to cope not only with their careers, but with other aspects of life. Psycho-social research also supports the notion that a mid-life career review may even precipitate a crisis if one finds a disturbing discrepancy between what one had hoped to accomplish by middle age, and what one has actually achieved. Intervention in terms of the career context might best be directed towards helping middle-aged men realistically assess their career aspirations in terms of their abilities and opportunities. For those experiencing boredom or job - related inertia, workshops and seminars which assist men in redefining or redirecting career goals could be helpful in their achieving greater satisfaction from their work. Lowenthal (1975) also addressed this problem with the suggestion that "in service organizations, business, industry, and the civil service, training facilities might be developed, so that the middle-aged men and women on all occupational levels can prepare for a second career if they so wish" (p. 245).

Developmental tasks within the family also present an area for adult educational programming. Unique to middle age is one's position between the older generation and the younger generation. The findings of this study suggest that middle-aged men in the generation squeeze feel burdened by

114

being responsible for both their parents and
their children. There is also a subtle psychological pressure, for in seeing one's parents age,
the middle-aged male may feel disturbed by what
is to come; likewise, one's children are a constant
reminder of the physical energy and future promise
which a middle-aged parent may no longer feel.
Havighurst (1952) has also delineated the two
important developmental tasks of this period as
having to adjust to aging parents and assisting
teenage children to become responsible and happy
adults. Learning activities dealing with the
physical and economic problems of aging parents,
as well as how to handle problems with one's
children--usually teenagers--would be helpful to
many middle-aged persons. Not to be overlooked
is the emotional dimension inherent in being the
middle generation. The conscious or unconscious
projection of oneself onto the aging parent or youthful teenager may for some middle-agers evoke resentment or tension which in turn affects interpersonal
relationships. Planned activities which assist
adults in first recognizing and then dealing with
such feelings would probably result in the better
handling of the economic and socially related
problems of one's parents and children.

        While there are no dramatic or sudden
physical changes for mid-life men, this study
found, as has most psycho-social research, that
changes in appearance can cause considerable concern. The awareness of aging manifested itself
in the protagonists' distress with their physical
deterioration--receding and greying hair, decreas-
ing muscle tone, and weight gain. Awareness of
their own aging was further accentuated by observing and fearing the deterioration of old age, while
at the same time not being able to sustain the
vitality of their youth. This leads several of
the protagonists into a desperate attempt at rejuvenation through sexual activity, which in turn
causes some to worry about a decline in sexual
functioning. Knox (1977) also states that "some
middle-aged adults acquire a value system that
glorifies youth and places extreme emphasis of

physical appearance and activity. Such people
often fear a physical and sexual decline" (p. 154).
In noting the interrelationship between aging and
sexual activity Knox (1977) writes:

> Some middle-aged men and women
> revolt against the loss of youth
> and engage in a 'second adolescesce.'
> Because of this the period around
> age forty is sometimes referred to
> as the 'dangerous age.' Men in
> particular tend to seek a younger
> woman as a lover or second wife....
> The results can be ironic if he is
> unable to meet her physical demands,
> and, instead of reducing his
> virility anxiety, the situation
> increases it. (p. 155)

By presenting workshops or seminars dealing with
physical aging and sexuality, adult educators and
counselors could intervene to help alleviate the
fears, misconceptions, and marital problems experienced by some men in mid-life.

Psychological functioning in middle-age
would also be a relevant source of educational programming. This study suggests that many middle-
aged men engage in a search for meaning characterized by a questioning of life and feelings that
one is losing bearings. Findings from psycho-
social research based on empirical studies and
clinical practice also supports the contention that
mid-life can be a period of introspection, self-
analysis, taking stock or life review. The interrelatedness of the several factors important to
middle age may combine to exert pressure and precipitate a crisis. One adult educator, Leon
McKenzie (n.d.), has proposed an educational program that addresses the theme of the mid-life
crisis. The "global objective," he states, is
that "at the conclusion of the program participants
will be able to identify characteristics of the
midlife crisis and techniques for the successful
negotiation of the crisis" (p. 8).

Indeed, McKenzie's program might well be prescribed for dealing with this study's findings concerning fragmentation and restructuring. As middle-aged men separate out the components of their lives for analysis and evaluation, educational intervention might be in the form of programs which explore goals for self-growth and development, ways to manage stress, and/or problem-solving techniques. Educational programs that can provide such self-help tools might facilitate the restructuring process so necessary for a person's future growth.

The specific findings of this study offer opportunities for program development in adult education. In general, adult educators might find it fruitful to program more in accordance with the developmental tasks and interests of various age groups. Indeed, Birren and Woodruff (1973) suggest that the purpose of education for adults should be to aid individuals in meeting the developmental tasks for their age level. With increasing age, participation in adult education drops (Knox, 1977; p. 184), a fact which might be in part attributed to the educator's failure to link adult development to educational opportunities. That such an approach is feasible is evidenced by efforts in the student services office of the Division of Continuing Education at the University of Kansas. Seminars and workshops have been offered which address the developmental tasks of various age groups. Workshops for middle-aged persons, for example, focus on many of the salient issues of mid-life: Mid-Career Workshop, Search for Meaning, Parenting to Teenagers, Relating to Aging Parents, and Stress Management (McCoy, 1977).

The voluntary nature of most adult education necessitates programming that is responsive to the needs and interests of a target population. Middle-aged men are in a period of life in which their concerns, developmental tasks, and personality development can be differentiated from young adulthood and old age. Findings about middle-aged men presented in this study can at least provide the adult educator with a starting point for planning meaningful educational experiences for this group.

REFERENCES

Albee, E. Who's afraid of Virginia Woolf?
New York: Atheneum, 1963.

Bellow, S. Herzog. New York: Viking Press,
1964.

Berger, M. Real and imagined worlds: The novel
and social science. Cambridge: Harvard
University Press, 1977.

Birren, J. E. & Woodruff, D. S., Human development
over the life span through education. In
P. Baltes, and K. W. Schaie (Eds.), Life span
developmental psychology: Personality and
socialization. New York: Academic, 1973.

Brim, O. G. Theories of the male mid-life crisis.
The Counseling Psychologist, 1976, 6(1), 2-8.

Bromley, D. B. The psychology of human aging.
Baltimore: Penguin, 1974.

Buhler, C. Psychology for contemporary living.
New York: Dell, 1968.

Butler, R. N. Age: The life review. Psychology
Today, 1971, 5, 29-58.

Bye, I. The mid-life crisis of two fictional
women: How personality can affect adjustment
to crisis. Unpublished paper, Indiana University, 1975.

Cameron, P. Age parameters of young adult, middle-
aged, old, and aged. Journal of Gerontology,
1969, 24, 201-202.

Cather, W. The professor's house. New York:
Random House, 1925.

Darkenwald, G. Field research and grounded theory. In H. Long (Ed.), Research methods in adult education. Washington, D.C.: Adult Education Association of the U.S.A., 1978.

Dreiser, T. Sister Carrie. New York: New American Library, 1961.

Eliot, T. S. The love song of J. Alfred Prufrock. In The complete poems and plays, 1909-1950. Newark: Harcourt Bruce & Co., 1958.

Erikson, E. Childhood and society. New York: Norton, 1950.

Erikson, E. Insight and responsibility. New York: Norton, 1964.

Erikson, E. Reflections on Dr. Borg's life cycle. Daedalus, Spring 1976, 105(2), 1-28.

Evans, R. I. Dialogue with Erik Erikson. New York: Harper and Row, 1967.

Fitzgerald, F. S. Tender is the night. New York: Charles Scribner's Sons, 1934.

Frenkel-Brunswik, E. Adjustments and reorientation in the course of the life span. In B. Neugarten (Ed.), Middle age and aging. Chicago: University of Chicago Press, 1968.

Freud, S. The interpretation of dreams. New York: Science Editions, Inc., 1961.

Friedman, E. A. Changing value orientations in adult life. In R. W. Burns (Ed.), Sociological backgrounds of adult education for adults. Syracuse: Center for the Study of Liberal Education for Adults, 1970.

Glaser, B. G. & Strauss, A. L. The discovery of grounded theory. Chicago: Aldine Publishing Co., 1967.

Gould, R. The phases of adult life: A study in developmental psychology. *The American Journal of Psychiatry*, November, 1972, *129*(5), 521-531.

Gutmann, D. L. An exploration of ego configurations in middle and later life. In B. Neugarten & Associates, *Personality in middle and late life*, New York: Atherton Press, 1964.

Havighurst, R. J. *Developmental tasks and education*. New York: David McKay, 1952.

Havighurst, R. J. Changing status and roles during the adult life cycle: Significance for adult education. In R. W. Burns (Ed.), *Sociological backgrounds of adult education*. Syracuse: Center for the Study of Liberal Education for Adults, 1970.

Havighurst, R. J. History of developmental psychology: Socialization and personality development through the life span. In P. Baltes & K. Warner Schaie (Eds.), *Life span development psychology*. New York: Academic Press, 1973.

Heller, J. *Something happened*. New York: Ballantine Books, 1975.

Hemingway, E. *The old man and the sea*. New York: Charles Scribner's Sons, 1952.

Howard, S. *They knew what they wanted*. 1924. In J. Mersand (Ed.), *Three plays about marriage*. New York: Washington Square Press, 1962.

Hunt, B. & Hunt, M. *Prime time*. New York: Stein and Day, 1975.

Jacques, E. Death and the mid-life crisis. *The International Journal of Psycho-Analysis*, 1965, *46*(4), 502-513.

Joyce, J. *A portrait of the artist as a young man*. New York: Viking Press, 1964.

Jung, C. The stages of life. In J. Campbell (Ed.), The portable Jung. New York: Viking Press, 1971.

Katchadourian, H. A. Medical perspectives on adulthood. Daedalus, Spring, 1976, 105(2), 29-56.

Kimmel, D. C. Adulthood and aging. New York: John Wiley and Sons, 1974.

Knox, A. B. Adult development and learning. San Francisco: Jossey-Bass, 1977.

Knox, A. B. (Ed.), Programming for adults facing mid-life change. San Francisco: Jossey-Bass, 1979.

Kohlberg, L. Continuities in childhood and adult moral development revisited. In P. Baltes & K. W. Schaie (Eds.), Life-span development psychology. New York: Academic Press, 1973.

Kubler-Ross, E. On death and dying. New York: Macmillan, 1969.

Kuhlen, R. G. Developmental changes in motivation during the adult years. In B. Neugarten (Ed.), Middle age and aging. Chicago: University of Chicago Press, 1968.

Lazerson, A. (Ed.). Psychology today: An introduction. New York: Random House, 1975.

Levinson, D. J. The psycho-social development of men in early adulthood and the mid-life transition. In Ricks, Thomas, and Roff (Eds.), Life history research in psycho-pathology. Minneapolis: University of Minnesota, 3, 1974.

Levinson, D. J. Periods in the adult development of men: Ages 18 to 45. The counseling psychologist, 1976, 6(1), 21-25.

Lewis, S. Babbitt. New York: New American Library, 1922.

Lidz, T. The person: His development throughout the life cycle. New York: Basic Books, 1968.

Lindauer, M. S. The psychological study of literature: Limitations, possibilities, and accomplishments. Chicago: Nelson-Hall, 1974.

Loughman, C. Novels of senescence. The Gerontologist, 1977, 17(1), 79-83.

Lowenthal, M. F. et al. Four stages of life. San Francisco: Jossey-Bass, 1975.

Marquand, J. P. Point of no return. Boston: Little, Brown and Company, 1949.

Marsick, V. Unpublished manuscript, n.d.

McCoy, V. Adult Life Cycle Change. Lifelong Learning: The Adult Years, 1977, 1(2), 14-18.

McKenzie, L. Analysis of Bildungsroman literature as a research modality in adult education: An inquiry. Adult Education, 1975, 25(4), 209-216.

McKenzie, L. Literary life-cycle research as an atypical research modality for adult education. Paper presented at the Adult Education Research Conference, Toronto, Canada, April 1976.

McKenzie, L. The mid-life crisis and educational programming. Indiana University, unpublished manuscript, n.d.

McKinney, F. Exploration in Bibliotherapy. Personnel and Guidance Journal, May 1977, 550-552.

McLeish, J. A. The Ulyssean adult. Toronto: McGraw Hill, 1976.

McMorrow, F. Midolescence: The dangerous years. New York: Quadrangle/New York Times Book Co., 1974.

Menninger, W. Bibliotherapy. Bulletin Menninger Clinic. 1937, 1, 263-274.

Merriam, S. Middle age: A review of the liter-
    ature and its implications for educational
    intervention. Adult education, 1978, 29(1),
    39-54.

Miller, A. Death of a salesman. New York:
    Penguin Books, 1949.

Neugarten, B. L. Personality in middle and late
    life. New York: Atherton Press, 1964.

Neugarten, B. L. Adult personality: Toward a
    psychology of the life cycle. Middle age and
    aging, Chicago: University of Chicago Press,
    1968a.

Neugarten, B. L. The awareness of middle age.
    Middle age and aging, Chicago, University of
    Chicago Press, 1968b.

Neugarten, B. L. Women's attitudes toward meno-
    pause. Middle age and aging, Chicago:
    University of Chicago Press, 1968c.

Neugarten, B. L. Personality change in late life:
    A developmental perspective. In C. Eisdorfer
    and M. P. Lawton (Eds.), The psychology of adult
    development and aging. Washington, D.C.:
    American Psychological Association, 1973.

Neugarten, B. L. Adaptation and the life cycle.
    The Counseling Psychologist, 1976, 6(1),
    16-120.

Newman, B. & Newman, P. Development through life:
    A psycho-social approach, Homewood, Ill.:
    Dorsey Press, 1975.

Peck, R. C. & Berkowitz, H. Personality and ad-
    justment in middle age. In B. Neugarten and
    Associates, Personality in middle and late
    life, New York: Atherton Press, 1964.

Peck, R. C. Psychological developments in the
    second half of life. In B. Neugarten (Ed.),
    Middle age and aging, Chicago: University of
    Chicago Press, 1968.

Plank, R. The emotional significance of imaginary beings: A study of the interaction between psychopathology, literature, and reality in the modern world, Springfield, Ill.: C. C. Thomas, 1968.

Pressey, S. L. Psychological development through the life span. New York: Harper & Row, 1957.

Rappoport, L. Adult development: faster horses... and more money. American Personnel and Guidance Journal, November 1976, 106-108.

Ricciardelli, R. M. King Lear and the theory of disengagement. The Gerontologist, Summer 1973, 148-152.

Rice, E. The adding machine. 1923. In H. Hatcher (Ed.) Modern American Dramas. New York: Harcourt, Brace and World, Inc., 1941.

Roen, P. R. Male sexual health. New York: William Morrow and Co., Inc., 1974.

Salinger, J. D. The catcher in the rye. Boston: Little, Brown and Co., 1951.

Sears, R. & Feldman, S. S. (Eds.), The seven ages of man. Los Altos: Kaufmann, 1973.

Sheehy, G. Passages: Predictable crisis of adult life. New York: E. P. Dutton & Co., 1976.

Shrodes, C., Van Gundy, J., & Husband, R. (Eds.), Psychology through literature: An anthology. New York: Oxford University Press, 1943.

Slotkin, J. S. Life course in middle age. Social forces, 1952, 33, 171-177.

Soddy, K. & Kidson, M. Men in middle life. Philadelphia: Lippincott, 1967.

Sohngen, M.   The experience of old age as depicted in contemporary novels.   The Gerontologist, 1977, 17(1), 70-77.

Troll, L.   Early and middle adulthood.   Monterey: Brooks/Cole, 1975.

Updike, J.   A month of Sundays.   Greenwich: Fawcett Publications, 1975.

Vaillant, G. E. & McArthur, C. C.   Natural history of male psychological health: The adult life cycle from 18-50.   Seminars in Psychiatry, 1974, 4(4), 415-427.

Vaillant, G. E.   Adaptation to life.   Boston: Little, Brown and Co., 1977a.

Vaillant, G. E.   How the best and the brightest came of age.   Psychology Today, September 1977b, 34-41, 107-110.

Wellek, R. & Warren, A.   Theory of literature. New York: Harcourt, Brace and Company, 1942.

Weyrauch, H. M.   Life after fifty: The prostatic age.   Los Angeles: Ward Ritchie Press, 1967.

Williams, T.   A streetcar named desire.   New York: The New American Library, 1947.

Williams, T.   The night of the iguana.   New York: The New American Library, 1961.

Wolfe, T.   You can't go home again.   New York: Harper & Row, 1940.

INDEX

Neugarten, B., 10, 13, 89, 90, 91, 92
The Night of the Iguana, 36, 44, 52, 59, 75, 84,
    102

Oedipus complex, 8, 9
Oedipus Rex, 8
Oppressive responsibility, 46-50

Parental pressure, 53-55
Peck, R., 96
Peer/spouse confirmation of aging, 33-36, 93, 94
Point of No Return, 33, 36
The Professor's House, 30, 33, 43, 75

Questioning of life, 40-42

Reordered time perspective, 29-31, 90
Restructuring, 28, 72, 77-84
    failure to restructure, 84-86
Ricciardelli, R., 7

Search for meaning in mid-life, 40-46, 71
    questioning of life, 40-42
    loss of bearings, 42-46
Sexual activity, 67-70
Shannon, 36, 44, 52, 59, 68, 75, 76, 84
Slocum, Bob, 29, 31, 32, 36, 38, 42, 43, 48, 49,
    52, 53, 55, 56, 57, 60, 61, 63, 69, 74, 76, 83,
    99
Slotkin, J., 91
Sohngen, M., 7
Something Happened, 29, 31, 36, 38, 99
St. Peter, Godfrey, 30, 33, 34, 39, 40, 43, 44, 49,
    51, 64, 75, 82

Tender is the Night, 27, 100
They Knew What They Wanted, 33, 66, 91, 102
Troll, L., 9

Vaillant, G., 93, 97, 98

Webber, G., 30, 35, 37, 41, 45, 54, 55, 66, 67, 83
"Wild Strawberries," 7